CROWDS and *RIOTS*

SOCIOLOGICAL OBSERVATIONS

series editor: JOHN M. JOHNSON, *Arizona State University*

"This new series seeks its inspiration primarily from its subject matter and the nature of its observational setting. It draws on all academic disciplines and a wide variety of theoretical and methodological perspectives. The series has a commitment to substantive problems and issues and favors research and analysis which seek to blend actual observations of human actions in daily life with broader theoretical, comparative, and historical perspectives. SOCIOLOGICAL OBSERVATIONS aims to use all of our available intellectual resources to better understand all facets of human experience and the nature of our society."

–John M. Johnson

Volumes in this series:

1. THE NUDE BEACH, by Jack D. Douglas and Paul K. Rasmussen, with Carol Ann Flanagan

2. SEEKING SPIRITUAL MEANING, by Joseph Damrell

3. THE SILENT COMMUNITY, by Edward William Delph

4. CROWDS AND RIOTS, by Sam Wright

5. THE MAD GENIUS CONTROVERSY, by George Becker

CROWDS
and
RIOTS
A Study in Social
Organization

Sam Wright

 SAGE PUBLICATIONS   Beverly Hills   London

Copyright © 1978 by Sage Publications, Inc.

For information address:

SAGE PUBLICATIONS, INC.
275 South Beverly Drive
Beverly Hills, California 90212

SAGE PUBLICATIONS LTD
28 Banner Street
London EC1Y 8QE

Printed in the United States of America

Library of Congress Cataloging in Publication Data

Wright, Sam.
    Crowds and riots.

    (Sociological observations ; v. 4)
    Includes bibliographical references and index.
    1. Crowds. 2. Riots. 3. Collective behavior.
4. Nonverbal communication. I. Title. II. Series.
HM281.W74   301.18'2   78-626
ISBN 0-8039-0995-0
ISBN 0-8039-0996-9 pbk.

FIRST PRINTING

CONTENTS

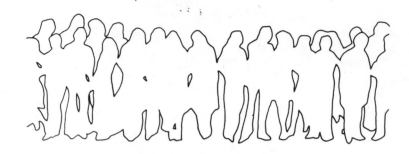

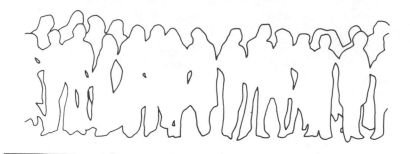

Situational collective behavior is a contrasting phenomena in an industrial society. It stands apart from the highly individualized interactions that dominate the bureaucratic social order. Village or tribal life with their routine communal gatherings are unknown to most readers of these words. The complexities of modern life have combined to relegate our collective interactions to non-routine situations. When we do gather together in one spatial/temporal setting, the contrast can be startling.

Under no other circumstance will one find, what I have come to call, the mix. This is a variegated, often exotic, and ever shifting blend of people. Our abstract conceptions of how society is composed come to life in crowds. Here we find simultaneously present and interacting with one another, people reflecting remarkably different status displays, ethnic groupings, modes of dress and demeanor, cultural signs and symbols, social classes, community actions, generations, styles of life, presentations of self, beauty and danger, group conflicts, ad infinitum.

To enter into a crowd is to become part of the dynamics of a unique reality. The outcome of these collective interactions vary from the most boringly mundane to collective panics and riots. This is a book based on my observations of crowds and riots. For details of how the participant observation was conducted, the methodology appendix is recommended. For now it is enough to say that over a three-year period, I took notes while sitting, walking, and running about in situations of collective behavior.

At the time of the research, this seemed to strike many people as an unusual activity in which to be engaged. "You mean you walk around in the middle of riots with pad and pen taking notes?" "Yes, that pretty well sums it up." "Man, you've got to be crazy!" "Well not exactly, I would say more curious than anything else. After all, no one before has ever systematically observed so much crowd behavior. So I'm curious to see what goes on."

There is a lot about which to be curious. Collective behavior consistently catches public interest. Yet public knowledge as to how collective interaction operates is seldom objectively or factually based. For example, last years' "riots" during New York City's Black Out were headlined in Time Magazine (July 25, 1977) as a "Night of Terror." Many respectable citizens, including the Mayor, echoed this characterization.

But what had actually taken place? Had people lost emotional control and become frenzied packs of crazed animals looting, raping, killing as a "night of terror" implies? No. A festive spirit of one giant Christmas party seems to have prevailed. Looting was often rationally organized, happily carried out, and frequently shared. Killing and raping was little in evidence. The image of the crowd behavior put forth by the press and politicians was inconsistent with what actually occurred. Unfortunately it is this image which shapes how publics interpret and react to these type of events.

Because cultural terms employed to describe collective activities are commonly selected for yellow journalism or political reasons, we do not know what behaviors they actually represent. As we saw during the time of the anti-Vietnam war demonstrations, collective behavior called a peaceful protest by one group would be labeled a riot by another group. What behavior does the term riot represent? What similarities are there between looting sprees in New York City and antiwar demonstrations in San Francisco? When power and not empirical fact is the determinant of how a label will be used, rational understanding of a phenomena becomes hopelessly clouded.

It is not idle whimsy to state that there is much to be curious about when studying crowd behavior. There is a real scholarly and social need for this type of information. This book is a serious effort to objectively report on and analyze some basic behaviors that I empirically found to be taking place in collective activities. In Chapter

One, there is a review of the works of others who have also given serious thought to these matters. Noticeably absent from this review are some major works dealing with crowds and riots. This exclusion reflects differences in levels of analysis. The basic questions that framed my field observations and analysis aimed at determining, "what collective interactions are actually taking place here and now, and unfolding over time?" and "how do these interactions operate or function?" Theoretical and ideological considerations as to, "why these behaviors took place," "what were the conditions that gave rise to them," or, "how do publics, press, police, politicians or organizations define the behaviors" — go beyond the intent of this study. Given that there is such limited agreement as to what are the behavioral referents of most collective behavior terms, these latter questions indeed seem somewhat premature. First in priority would seem to be the gathering of knowledge as to what is transpiring.

The interactions that I came to focus on for study are basic to all situations of collective assembly. That is groups interacting with other groups. Groups in collective behavior are seldom the highly formalized creations found in the institutional order. Instead they are emergent, ever evolving, relatively ephemeral entities.

In observing these groups, their spatial characteristics seemed to provide the most sound empirical basis for description. The spatial shape or form of groups as these reflect the groups activities, the zones of space that extend out from groups and how these are used, the division of labor among groups and the resultant spatial system of interaction are the observed phenomena that is presented and analyzed. Since these spatial relations are oriented to, used, and read for information, nonverbally, then nonverbal interaction and communication is a theme underlying each chapter.

In sum, the following should contain something of relevance to those interested in collective behavior, spatial interaction, form and form perception, nonverbal communication, social control or social disruption, and the processes by which situated meanings come to be assigned to collective behavior.

My deepest gratitude goes to some dear people. These people have not only been academically supportive but steadfast friends as well. I am truly overwhelmed by such fortune. John Johnson as a colleague and editor for Sage, has been both champion and advisor. His most valuable and insightful comments never failed to include the statement that, "editing should not interfere with what the author wants to say."

Richard Morris and Donna VerSteeg simply made this book possible. Jim Bishop, Jerry Schutte, Clark Molsted, and Phil Davis took their valuable time to read the original manuscript and comment. Gentlemen, I remain in your debt. In a very special one woman category, is my sister-in-law, Sandi Wright, who designed the figures for the book and kept this effort together through some pretty rough times. May happiness always be yours, Sandi. The tasks of proofing and index construction were brought up to professional standards through the meticulous efforts of David Korn and family, a most pleasant experience.

—S. W.

DEFINING THE PROBLEM
Introduction to a Problem

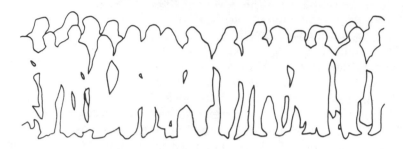

Dispatch, this is Jenkins.

Go ahead Jenkins!

There are three of us over here by the canyon's edge on _____'s private farm. We're having a hard time keepin' 'em people out. Some joker been tellin' 'em that it's O.K. to come in here. Can you get some of the Sheriff's men to help us out?

10-4. We'll see what we can do. Meanwhile, you do the best you can until backup arrives.

(14 minutes later)

DISPATCH! This is JENKINS!

Go ahead.

IT'S TOO LATE NOW! We could handle the individuals but, a MOB HAS BROKEN DOWN THE FENCE. They've run across the field . . . a regular wall of people! And now, thar lined up and shovin' one another, five to ten people deep, along the canyon rim! Some of 'um are sure goin' to be pushed or fall over the edge! It's just plain crazy! There's motorcycles drivin' about here, everywhere, and more people are comin' in all the time. I don't see how they expect us to handle it.

10-4. I don't see how they could expect you to handle that, either. Look! If you think it's safe, try to stay in the area and stop them from setting any fires. If not, get the hell on out of there[1].

This is a book about crowds and crowd interactions. In contradistinction to the majority of scholarly or popular writings on crowds, the following is based on research actually conducted in the field. For the most part, it draws upon personal observations (participant observation) of various types of crowds and riots. When accounts other than the investigator's are employed as data, only those that are from direct, eyewitness reports are used. The challenge of this research was to observe the ongoing interactions taking place throughout the developmental career of each crowd.

This study began as a general exploration of these naturally occurring phenomena. After a few months, the investigation was focused on the nonverbal interaction which appeared as a basic and constant factor in crowd behavior. Such nonverbal phenomena as individual and collective gesturings, rates and directions of movement, body and facial cues of odor, color and sweat became those aspects of the empirical world carved out for detailed observation. After observing these phenomena for a period of time, the investigation was further focused on a specific aspect of the nonverbal interaction — the spatial relationship between individuals and groups in crowds. From these observations of the spatial relations came the discovery/creation of the subject of this study: **Spatial** or **Group Forms.**

"Spatial forms" are a genuine sociological phenomena. They are *the collective configurations or patterns which emerge out of crowd members' distribution in space.* These forms belong to no individual, but are the interactional product of individuals standing in relation to one another. Therefore, rather than looking at the spatial zones or distances surrounding one individual, the spatial distribution of the various *shapes of subgroups and of the whole collectivity* is the prime "object" of attention.

Spatial forms were selected for study out of a large range of other possibilities. The selection was made on the basis of real world interactional importance. In crowd situations, group forms (unlike other verbal and nonverbal behaviors) have a continual, simultaneous visibility to those collectively assembled. Because of this presence, and other reasons to be discussed, group forms come to play a continual role in ongoing collective interaction.

By studying group forms, larger problems, such as the basis of coordination of collective activities, can be addressed. This latter, more general problem, will lie behind the development of our arguments as to the role of spatial forms in collective behavior. Together they constitute the problem to which this book is directed — or — *How do crowd members create and use group forms in nonverbal interac-*

tion as a mechanism for coordinating and carrying out collective activities?

Some of the aspects of forms that this book is concerned with are: (1) What are some of the recurring forms to be found among crowds? (2) What is the role of forms in the nonverbal communication that takes place in crowd situations? (3) What is the relationship between the collective form that a group has and the activities its members are engaged in? (4) How does the form that the group has affect the activities that produced it?

Chapter 1 has three sections:

Section 1 provides a general review of the theoretical literature on collective behavior indicating its assumptions regarding nonverbal interaction.

Section 2 reviews the empirical literature on crowds. The emphasis is on those research findings which contribute most directly to our understanding of crowd nonverbal interactions.

Section 3 presents a brief look at the concept of form as it has been researched and used from psychology to architecture.

SECTION 1: WHAT OTHERS HAVE SAID: A REINTERPRETATION

Whether as a direct object of study or as a process about which assumptions are made, the question: "How do crowd members coordinate and carry out collective interactions?" is an ever present problem to the student of collective behavior. In their latest book, *Collective Behavior,*[2] Turner and Killian see this question as being central to any basic understanding of the phenomena: "The task of studying collective behavior involves identification of the source of this coordination."[3] The following review of what others have said about crowds selects out for attention relevant statements and findings pertaining to coordination in crowd interactions.

These statements shall be organized using a basic schema suggested by Turner and Killian. They hold that authors can be differentially classified as being either **contagion, convergence,** or **emergent norm** theorists.[4] We shall come to see that, despite theoretical differences, there is at least one underlying commonality among these authors' works. Much of what has been written about collective behavior can be understood, i.e., reinterpreted, as attempts to describe processes of nonverbal interaction.

A word of caution is appropriate. The following elaboration is selective in emphasis and in argument. Although verbal interaction in collective behavior is only tangentially discussed, its omission is not intended to imply a one-sided view of communication in collective assemblies. In fact, the opposite is the case. What is offered here is meant to balance those interpretations that deal only with verbal interaction.

Previous theorists have properly noted the importance in collective behavior of speeches, leadership harangues, verbal keynoting, rumors moving through crowds and riots, and small group discussions. What has not been noted, however, are those most frequent occasions in collective interaction where there is no verbal interaction taking place, and those occasions where, although verbal interaction occurs, there is also relevant nonverbal interaction.

The below is an examination that has two goals. One, is the demonstration, by selection from prior writings, that theorists are often describing the nonverbal interaction in collective behavior, while stating that processes other than the nonverbal are at work. The second goal is to enumerate what these processes are and how they are inappropriately used to gloss over nonverbal interactions.

IMITATION/CONTAGION THEORISTS

In 1896, Gustave Le Bon wrote *The Crowd*.[5] This popular book was one of the first efforts to deal with the phenomena as a subject worthy of serious analysis. It was also one of the first studies to present the thesis that two processes in conjunction account for the "extreme" nature of crowd behavior. These were the "group mind, collective mind, or crowd mind" and the interactional/psychological processes of "suggestion, imitation, or emotional contagion."[6]

Stating that people act differently in crowds from the way they do in settings of one-to-one interactions, Le Bon held that this was a consequence of the appearance of the "collective mind."[7] He believed that this unconsciously came into being whenever large numbers of people gather together. The group mind was characterized by homogeneity of feeling, thought and action that is an expression of crowd members' being reduced to the lowest common denominator of their collective unconscious.

Le Bon's thesis was that leveling, absorption, and the individual's loss of control to a collective mind, provided the conditions for crowd interactions to become dominated and guided by processes of suggestion, imitation, and emotional contagion. Le Bon did not rigorously distinguish between these concepts nor specifically define them. Instead, he relied on their face value meanings to explain the irrational behavior he felt occurred in crowds.

Crowd members were described as imitating one another's behavior rather than taking independent reasoned courses of action. "Man, like animals has a natural tendency to imitation."[8] Members were held to be subject to being caught up in or catching by contagion, the prevalent emotional excesses of the group. They were also seen as accepting, unquestioningly, whatever suggestions were keynoted in the group. In summary, Le Bon believed that crowd members appear to be guided neither by rational discourses, emotional control, nor reflexive behavior.

Many of Le Bon's basic concepts were used to explain collective coordination of behavior in crowds by several later writers. Before discussing their works, a few introductory comments are in order. With these comments we will show how these writers, and Le Bon, try to account for nonverbal interaction with inappropriate frame works. Imitation and emotional contagion are particularly germane concepts for this task.

In large part the homogeneity of action that Le Bon felt described crowd behavior, relies on an implicit statement on nonverbal interaction. If one person takes an independent action, the mass of the others are said "to see" this and to then imitate or copy this behavior. This "seeing" and the knowing that accompanies it are based upon a visually oriented, nonverbal interaction. The collective coordinated behavior that results is a consequence of this nonverbal interaction.

Contagion, likewise, is described in terms of nonverbal interaction. It is direct or face-to-face picking up of the sentiments of others — as if one were in a "dream" state or "hypnotized."[9]

> Ideas, sentiments, emotions, and beliefs possess in crowds a contagious power as intense as that of microbes. This phenomena is very natural, since it is observed even in animals when they are together in number. Should a horse in a stable take to biting his managers hand the other horses in the stable will imitate him. A panic that has seized on a few sheep will soon extend to the whole flock. In the case of men collected in a crowd, all emotions are rapidly contagious, which explains the suddenness of panics.[10]

Again, members are being held to be imitating through exposure to and direct knowing of (but not through verbal conceptualization of) the emotional states or appearances of others. Crowd coordination, in part, is conceived as resting on the resulting shared sentiment.

While Le Bon made suggestions all around the idea of perceiving and knowing through our senses other than verbally, he got no further. Popular scholarly ways of ordering the world at that time — the collective consciousness, the collective unconscious, mass hypnosis — tended to explain and mystify without creating any need for a more explicit analysis of how such processes worked. For the next twenty-five years, most writers on the subject fared little better. The later work of Edward Ross (1905), William McDougall (1920), and of R. Park and E. Burgess (1921) built upon the basic thesis of Le Bon.[11]

Thus, by the 1920s, a perspective with shared assumptions about crowds had appeared, that, with modification, is still held by the Imitation/Contagion school of theorists today. This approach has an image of crowd behavior as being emotional and irrational as compared to noncrowd behavior. Accompanying this imagery are accounts explaining the irrationality of crowds in terms of processes of contagion, imitation, and suggestibility. The Imitation/Contagion approach differs from Le Bon only in that the underlying cause of the crowd's character is changed from that of a mystic group mind to that of an empirically observable effect of people gathering together. Mass hypnosis is dropped from the list of explanatory processes, and these processes themselves are treated more as interactional phenomena than as psychic or instinctual ones.[12]

Two later presentations of this position are of particular interest for the development of our argument. Both Blumer,[13] writing in 1939 on contagion processes, and Couch, writing in 1970 on imitation processes,[14] have implicit but detailed nonverbal interactional explanations for coordinations in crowds. Blumer moves directly into a nonverbal interactional description of crowd behavior with his theory of circular reaction:

> Circular reaction refers to a type of interstimulation wherein the response of one individual reproduces the stimulation that has come from another individual, and in being reflected back to this individual reinforces the stimulation. Thus, the interstimulation forms a circular form in which individuals reflect one another's states of feelings and in doing so, intensify this feeling.[15]

Using the analogy between people in crowds and cattle in a herd, Blumer goes on to say:

> The expression of fear through bellowing, breathing and the movement of the body, induces the same feeling in the case of others . . . and intensifies this emotional state in one another.[16]

In this passage is ample evidence of Blumer's belief in the nonverbal nature of the proposed causal processes and his equating of the nonverbal with the irrational. For Blumer, this circular reaction process is different from normal interactional processes. Under his thesis, people govern their activities, in noncrowd interaction, via an interpretive (reflexive and rational) process.

He says the lack of interpretive behavior in crowds is reflected in their emotional and irrational character.

Couch (1970), while arguing that interpretive processes are not the exclusive domain of noncrowd behavior,[17] does hold that: "Within collective behavior episodes the bondness or unity of a group rest primarily upon parallel role taking,"[18] and "in parallel role-taking the absence of distinctive perspective minimizes interpretive responses."[19] Again, the imagery of crowd behavior is that of being primarily nonrational.

Since he defines crowds as essentially nonrational, the problem remains to explain how coordination of collective activities occur. Couch returns to parallel role-taking. Explaining and defining the concept, he states that it

. . . often involves one actor making the same response on a covert level that another makes on an overt level . . .[20]

Concerted action necessitates that members of a social unit align or fit together their activities. In some situations (marching demonstrations) the alignment is parallel. That is, members of a unit exhibit identical or similar behavior.[21]

In other words, the dominant process of coordination of crowds is that of imitation. The knowledge that guides these actions is obtained, for the most part, nonverbally or through "visual monitoring." This allows immediate parallel or imitation response of members to one another, because "visual monitoring can be simultaneously reciprocal, i.e., each participant simultaneously noting the activities of others."[22]

From Le Bon to the present time, there have been collective behavior theorists who share certain assumptions about crowd behavior. These Imitation/Contagion theorists have been of special interest here, as they tended to describe the actual processes of crowd coordination as it occurred through some facet of nonverbal interaction. But, as a group, they likewise interpreted these nonverbal processes as being basically irrational or emotional, or nonreflexive imitation. Consequently, they have failed to deal systematically with nonverbal interaction qua nonverbal interaction. The problem seems to be that, once having defined crowd behavior in general as being irrational, imitative or noninterpretive, one is blocked from pursuing the possibilities that nonverbal interaction occurring therein can be as interpretively based as verbal behavior.

CONVERGENT THEORISTS

A different theoretical position on crowds developed in the 1920s. These writers have appropriately become known as the Convergent Theorists. Beginning first with Freud, we shall trace out the general movement of this position into contemporary times.

Addressing Le Bon's thesis, Freud (1922)[23] challenged the idea of crowds being dominated by a group mind. He rejected contagion, imitation, and suggestion as being the causal or determining processes in crowd interaction. Yet he does go on to say, using a nonverbal reference that "there is no doubt that something exists in us which, when we become aware of signs of an emotion in someone else, tends to make us fall into the same emotion."[24]

And what is this something? Freud stated that there is a "frustration relationship" between crowd members and their leaders. This produces their "primitive" behavior. The thesis can be briefly stated: Because there are too many crowd members to permit each to possess the desired leader individually, frustrated members "revert" to identifying with the leaders' actions and suggestions. In other words, if an individual cannot 'have' the desired object, then he trys to 'be' the same as the object. As each person identifies with the leader, individually, then any rational or irrational signs by the leader will be followed by simultaneous individual reactions. This also, in part, produces the homogeneity of behavior said to characterize the crowd. People are not dominated by a group mind, rather they become "group individuals."[25]

In 1924, with his book, *Social Psychology,*[26] F. Allport introduced another psychological interpretation of crowd behavior. This approach differs from the Freudian model. But it and the Freudian models contain common elements of a convergence thesis. The primary characteristics of the convergence model, as distinct from the imitation/contagion school's are: (1) the rejection of any unique group level explanation for crowd behavior; (2) the acceptance of the idea that individuals essentially behave no differently alone than in a crowd, "only more so"; and (3) the belief that there is a tendency for crowds to be composed of individuals of like minds who have *converged* into an area for reasons of previously established interests. In the academic realm, these assumptions came to be shared and most actively developed by psychologists, psychological behaviorists, and sociological exchange theorists.

Psychologists have come to dominate the convergence approach, and Allport was one of its earliest and most powerful spokesmen. Therefore, let us consider: (a) how he differs from the Freudian view, (b) what is still shared with the imitation/contagion theorists, and (c) what is the significant role of nonverbal interaction in this position. Though agreeing with the Freudians in terms of the assumptions of convergence, Allport suggested different dynamics govern actual crowd interactions. This caused him to reject such Freudian ideas as projection and identification, and the necessary role of the leader.

In their place, he proposed that a process of stimulus-response is at work:

> The harangue of the leader, or similar stimuli common to all, increase this preparation to the point of breaking forth. The command or first movement of some individuals toward the act prepared affords the stimulus for release. Finally, when action and emotion are away, the sights and sounds of each other's reactions facilitates and increases further the response of each.[27]

From this we see that the basic imagery of the crowd as "irrational" is also an assumption of this position as something that characterizes the crowd and as such, as something that needs to be explained.

The stimulus-response process itself is of particular interest in terms of our argument about the important part nonverbal interaction plays in all theories of collective behavior. Allport, in elaborating this process, stated that: exposure to a common stimulus, results in a common response, and those who have converged into an area already share *predisposed similar tendencies and interests for action.* In the crowd setting, members become aware of the stimulus responses of others through "sights and sounds." The total process is referred to as *social facilitation.*

This involves knowing the feelings, thoughts, and reactions of others through such nonverbal stimuli as "facial expressions, gestures, shouts, hisses, and murmurs."[28] Again, this time from a totally different perspective, we encounter agreement about the fundamental importance of nonverbal interaction in crowd behavior. Without, in any way, making the nonverbal something to be understood or explained on its own terms, it is offered up as a crucial factor in accounting for collective coordination of actions in crowds.

The later "convergence-oriented" work of Miller and Dollard (1941)[29] offers little change from Allport's position. But two sources of differing interpretations, within the convergence framework, do develop. One comes out of a "Parsonian" approach and the other out of the over-rationalistic tendency of exchange theory.

The sociologist, Neil Smelser, in his instant classic, *Theory of Collective Behavior* (1962),[30] maintains that crowd members are motivated by and organize their actions within crowds via "generalized hostile beliefs." People with these beliefs converge into an area with already established symbols of villainy and rigid interpretations of the social situation. While leaning towards the "irrational" imagery of crowd behavior, Smelser does not develop a position detailing the processes of crowd interaction. Instead, he concentrates on explaining the structural stages that lead to the crowd appearing in the first place. Though Smelser's Parsonian model of crowd behavior steps outside of the psychological tradition of convergence theorists, he continues to share their basic assumptions and imagery of crowd behavior. As with other theorists, there is recognition by example but not in theory of the important role of nonverbal interaction. An example is Smelser's comments on panic:

> Communication, through either word or gesture, of a common assessment of the situation is apparent. Sometimes the fact that someone starts to run in a certain direction constitutes an affective definition of that situation.[31]

The point is that a man's act of running, without a verbal definition of the situation, is held to be, in and of itself, a sufficient source of nonverbal communication to set others into flight.

The "exchange theory" variant of convergence theory is firmly within the psychological/convergence camp. The difference is nonetheless dramatic. With a theoretical statement by Katz (1940)[32] and a laboratory experiment by Mintz (1951)[33] there began a movement towards a basic modification in the imagery of the crowd. As Brown put it in a 1954 article reviewing the arguments for imputing some rationality to crowd behavior:

> The famous and mad rush for the fire exit is a fairly rational reaction when others have stepped out of line and threaten to block your way.[34]

In 1974, this cognitive challenge to the traditional imagery of irrationality was pursued to its most extreme conclusion by a sociological exchange theorist. Berk (1974),[35] claiming to have discovered total rationality in all crowd behavior, criticizes preceding writers for having insisted on seeing crowd behavior otherwise. For reasons other than its unique over-rationalized model of man, this article will be covered in some detail in the next section. For now, let us simply use it as a springboard into a discussion of the third and final strand in the theoretical literature on collective behavior. This group of writers we shall call the normative/interactionists. These men share few of the assumptions or little of imagery about crowd behavior of either the Imitation/Contagion theorist or the convergence theorist. They do, however, share with Katz, Berk et al. the belief that not all crowd behavior is irrational.

EMERGENT NORMS

To trace out the roots of this contribution to collective behavior theory would require going back to all the theorists mentioned and then some. For what this theory's originators, Turner and Killian, have done in their major works (Turner and Killian, 1956,[36] Turner, 1964,[37] Turner and Killian, 1972[38]) is to select and build from pieces of insight scattered throughout the literature. The two central elements in their position to be dealt with here pertain to the crucial role of interaction and emergent norms in collective situations.

McDougall, Park, and Burgess stressed the fact that regardless of how you wished to characterize crowds, those qualities that are attributed to them must be products of the interaction taking place within the collective assembly or in terms of the collectivity in interaction with its environment. Turner and Killian used this insight while avoiding many of the pitfalls of the convergence and Imitation/Contagion theorists. By 1956 enough empirical evidence was in to clearly demonstrate that crowd behavior is:

1. *Not homogeneous;* that is, any particular crowd was likely to contain substantial numbers of different attitudes and behaviors and there is almost always a different degree of participation in the on-going actions ranging from opposition to passivity to full engagement.

2. *Crowd behavior is not inherently rational or irrational;* this is true in that crowd members, by all accounts, appear to be interacting interpretively. They are not necessarily carried away by either mass hypnosis or hysteria. They are, in fact, acting according to differences

in a situation in terms of which these actions frequently have a sense of being appropriate.

3. *Crowd behavior is not guided by nonnormative factors,* that is, while primary types of interaction perhaps lack the type of complexity of collective interactions, both are guided by and constrained by norms.

In pursuing the question of norms, Turner and Killian make their most significant contribution towards understanding collective behavior. Drawing upon the observations of writers from Le Bon to Blumer, that crowds lacked the traditional normative control of routinized groups, they asked, "can it be said that norms exist in a collectivity?"[39] The answer to this question is in part derived from the Asch studies. In this series of laboratory experiments,[40] individual subjects were shown to conform to emergent group norms that were not traditionally or culturally pre-given. Applying this understanding to crowds, Turner and Killian suggest that situationally derived norms of behavior emerge out of the collective interactions therein, ordering and structuring that self-same behavior.

Within the concept of "emergent norms", behavior inconsistent with the interpretations of the contagion/imitation and convergence theses can now be explained. Imitation/Contagion theorists were unable to account for how once the "circular reaction" of emotional contagion got started, it ever managed to stop before all were reduced to a state of emotional frenzy. The answer suggested by emergent norm theorists is that norms emerge limiting and determining the situated degree of fear, anger, excitability, etc., that are appropriate to that time and place.

Convergence theorists, on the other hand, had been hard put to explain the findings that: (1) there do not appear to be any discernible, consistent characteristics among those who take part in riots (i.e., no apparent convergence of similar types of people appears to be taking place)[41] or (2) to explain the fact that in the course of a crowd's history, extremely contradictory actions occur at different times (e.g., a mob that has been destroying all opposition in its path, lets one unarmed man stop them.)[42]

The emergent norm position points to the lack of a "predisposing to riot convergence" and indicates the developmental, interactionally produced nature of crowd behavior. To understand why a crowd "did" something, one must know what were the processes and normative definitions of the situation which led up to the "doing." With this knowledge, one can see how contradictory courses of action can come out of the same group of people over time, because they change their definitions of what should be done.

In summary, the image of the crowd undergoes a major and significant change under the emergent norm position. Members are held to be interacting interpretively with one another and their environment. Whether or not the decisions and actions taken or the definitions of the situation accepted as appropriate, are rational or irrational is held to be a value judgment — it depends upon whether one likes or dislikes the actions, and/or their consequences. Interactional processes occur in and are the means by which the crowd activities develop. If in the course of a group's career, members, through interaction, become highly emotionally involved, emergent norms will develop along with the emergent behavior. These norms will prescribe and proscribe the permissible levels of emotion and types of behavior. In a short period, the emergent norm position has become the orienting framework for several scholars. Quarantelli, Hundley, and McPhail are three whose works have made use of this perspective.

My own initial approach to studying crowd behavior was based on the assumptions and understandings of the interactionist/emergent norm position. But, as with the other approaches, this one makes use of the role of nonverbal interaction in crowds, while leaving it out of any serious theoretical consideration. For example, this passage from Turner and Killian assumes nonverbal communication occurs in its discussion of expressive crowds:

> The person who would ordinarily be inhibited from dancing in the street, shouting his joy, and embracing strangers may feel free to do so when he sees others disregarding the usual norms of restraint and dignity. A spirit of competition develops in the expressive crowd, although it is a friendly competition. The extravagant expressions by some members seem to encourage others to outdo them in outburst.[43]

Even "milling" which at first encounter appears to be a passing recognition of the nonverbal is defined otherwise: "More importantly, milling becomes primarily a verbal process."[44]

As a consequence of such definitions, the emergent norm position is also open for criticism. The problem of "how coordination of actions takes place in a large collectivity" is dealt with by Turner and Killian via the idea of emergent norms. But, if members of a collective assembly are jointly acting in terms of a shared norm, how do they come to share these norms, how do they find out what they are? In other words, what are the processes through which the ongoing definition of the situation is communicated throughout an assembly?

For Turner and Killian, rumor transmission is the mechanism via which collective definitions of the situations are produced and communicated in crowds; i.e., verbal communication. To support this contention, a plethora of laboratory, small group, and diffused crowd studies are quoted, which all point to the significance of rumor for bringing definitional order to events of this kind. Despite this array of support, my own research raises a fundamental, empirical question about the ability of rumor to account for rapid changes in a crowd's direction and changes in action:

> . . . people were running in a pell-mell, pandemonium effort to get out of the reach of the advancing police. Those furthest away encountered auto traffic on a cross street. Some members moved to the right, paralleling the traffic. Those who came behind, followed, even though the way was totally open to the left as well and many people were actually closed to that avenue of escape.
> The police stopped their pursuit at the corner. Seeing this we, who had moments before been in full disarray, stopped, turned and began a cautious, slow, yelling and jeering return towards the officers.
> (Notes made later, at home):
> The crowd actions of today were, at many points, occurring at too rapid a pace for rumors to have been even a small factor. During one phase of the activities, 2,000 plus people changed direction twice and twice changed the nature of their activities — all within a minute and a half. Hardly enough time for guiding rumors to have swept through this many people. Significantly, there was also a complete absence of any verbal keynoting.[45]

While my own research has found rumor to be very important to crowd activity, as emergent norm theorists state, it also supports the criticism that it is not sufficient to explain many situations of nonverbal coordination of collective activities. It is the thesis of my position that the processes of nonverbal interactions, while often complementary to rumor, are essentially an independent element in the explanation of the coordination of collective activities.

The next short section is a review of the works on collective behavior which specifically note the relevance of some aspect of nonverbal interaction in crowds. The reasons for not including any of these efforts in this section is that, unlike the preceding, the following works are not large theoretical statements. The point being that, while a small but growing number of writers are turning more of their attention to the role of spatial factors, gesture, proximities, etc. in crowd interaction, there has not yet appeared any major attempt to either incorporate these into a theoretical orientation or to construct a summary and overall theoretical statement about them.

SECTION 2: THE CONTRIBUTION OF CONTEMPORARY RESEARCHERS

Since the nonverbal has not yet received any systematic theoretical treatment within the field of collective behavior, references to it as an element in crowd interactions tend to be more suggestive than systematically organized. This makes systematic reporting on them especially difficult. The imaginative article by Fisher,[46] demonstrates this problem.

Seeking to develop a conceptual vocabulary for describing and analyzing demonstrations, Fisher examines what he calls the "objective structures of the gatherings."[47] By this he is, in part, referring to ". . . micro-ecological features such as 'areas,' 'foci,' 'boundaries,' 'stages,' and 'edges.'" These are presented as analytic labels to be attached to various aspects of physical and relational space in crowds. Thus, Fisher sees these elements of nonverbal interaction as constituting extremely important features of crowds and crowd interaction.

He also discusses the manner in which certain role performers communicate their roles and manipulate others via their body movements:

> Newsmen move quite differently than police. They make themselves small and try to slip between members of the crowd . . . the other style is to let the T.V. cameramen lead and use the bulk of his camera . . . to open a path.[48]

Finally, Fisher makes a passing observation:

> . . . crowds are extremely fluid scenes . . . In the course of persons in the crowd engaging in their business (protesting, meeting friends, arresting, etc.) the configuration of the gathering consistently flows from one shape to another. In some sense, the essence of a thing called a "crowd" is just a spontaneous, unstable flow.[49]

While there is agreement herein about the importance of a crowd's configuration, the implications of this being rather random, "spontaneous," state of affairs are seriously challenged in this text.

Fisher's attention to as well as empirical grounding of his analysis in natural events, via participant observation, is a rare phenomena in collective behavior. One other student, Clark McPhail,[50] has made serious efforts to study crowds in their natural settings. Possibly as a consequence he, too, has come to deal with nonverbal interaction. Of interest are his comments on focused vs. diffused assemblies as McPhail advances beyond the original ideas as presented by Woolbert.

In 1916, Woolbert[51] stated that crowd activities could be separated into two phases: polarized — all members' attention given to one focus; and nonpolarized — interactions characterized by many clusters of face-to-face interactions. This observation has been passed basically unaltered through the next fifty years of writings on the crowd until McPhail puts forth two elaborations. First, he makes the point that an "audience" type crowd can be described on the basis of its career of shifting from being diffused (nonpolarized) to focused (polarized). Then he indicates how this shifting has important effects in terms of: (a) how people visually read what state an affair is in (e.g., the **audience formation stage** involves much small group orientation with heads turned towards one another); and (b) how people know what stage the proceedings have reached (e.g., a **focused assembly** is visible as an event is well underway).[52] This leads to the second suggestion that there are interactional effects of a collectivity focusing when not in fixed seats. There is an increased density in crowds as members assume "side-to-side and face-to-back" arrangements. This in turn results in:

> . . . (a) a restriction of the amount of physical movement in which the individual can engage (b) a restriction of the individual's total range of vision, i.e., predominantly straight ahead with restricted peripheral or lateral vision; (c) a restriction of the number of proximate others with whom an individual can talk, viz., to those on his immediate right and left. These increased restrictions should vary with the location of the individual within the focused assemblage . . .[53]

Stark et al. have done work that is an empirically grounded study of actual riot processes and is also more than just a generalization from one incident.[54] They mapped 1,850 incidents recorded in the Watts' Riot. The plotting of these instances was done in terms of spatial-temporal location. These revealed that the diffusion of riot behavior through the 46.5 square miles was not: (1) from contiguous area to contiguous area, and (2) that there was a daily cycle of riot activity rather than a series of stages of development. These observations and findings are primarily derived out of the direct, nonverbal observing of films taken of the riot. This research is an outstanding example of what can be accomplished when collective forms are used as the focus of study.

Most of the remaining studies on crowds study one incident — a case study — and the observations and analysis are not built on ongoing processes. Perhaps because of this, they also do not contribute directly to any additional understanding of nonverbal communication. Two exceptions to this trend are worth mention.

In a paper on crowds, Carl Couch[55] draws extensively upon the realm of the nonverbal to describe the processes of "association in collective behavior." These processes are stated to include "monitoring"[56] (how a situation is read visually and audibly); "alignment"[57] (how parallel behavior develops nonverbally); and "acknowledgement"[58] (how crowd members come to nonverbally understand that they are not subject to claims of having to acknowledge responsibility for their actions).

Unfortunately, as interesting as Couch's article is in terms of nonverbal communication, he uses the imagery of crowds dominated by homogenous, undifferentiated behavior in his study. Thus, the mechanism of crowd coordination suggested are limited to those cases where this might be the case. Furthermore, the dynamics of association in the end turns into a restatement (albeit an interesting one) of a Contagion/Imitation view of crowd behavior.

The other exception is an article by Berk[59] based on a case study of one incident of crowd activity. In discussing and analyzing the details of this incident, Berk points to the importance of nonverbal interaction. He described how the building of a barricade across a vehicle thoroughfare is a situationally produced change in the environment. The barricade is seen as forcing people to deal with this obstruction in terms of its meaning implications as well as in terms of its creating a physical passage problem.

Berk notes the role of a crowd's physical arrangement in space:

> First, a crowd's shape affects the visibility of crowd member activity. For example, a crowd which weaves through several city blocks will prevent many crowd members from seeing any action around the corner. Each crowd member's view will depend on higher location in relation to acting people. Consequently, not only will some crowds have structures, which affect overall (aggregate) visibility, but crowd members may have differing abilities to see.[60]

Thus, Couch and Berk, as distinct from most other theoretical/empirical article writers on crowd behavior, explicitly address the need to take into account various aspects of nonverbal interaction. In doing so they reflect the slow, but growing awareness of this element in all human interactions.

This section would not be complete without a mention of Milgram and Toch's chapter: "Collective Behavior: Crowds and Social Movement."[61] This is true not only because their efforts preceded and more thoroughly presented most of the concepts advanced by the authors noted above, but, more importantly, because they formally recognized and discussed shape as an "elementary feature of the crowd." Their discussion centers on the "ring" as a shape that unimpeded crowds develop "naturally."

> . . . If individuals are randomly distributed over a flat surface in a starting situation, a point of common interest in the same thing creates a crowd tending toward circularity. The circular arrangement is not accidental, but serves an important function. It permits the most efficient arrangement of individuals around a point of common focus. For experimental purposes, an ideal ring can be created by dragging and object of interest from the ocean and onto a populated beach. A treasure chest will suffice; a circular ring will form around it.
>
> Nature abhors a square crowd. A crowd builds in the form of accretions to the initial circular core. Even when a rings grows to be many layers thick, the circular shape tends to prevail.[62]

Next, the various subparts or features of the ring are labeled, e.g., outer boundary — the outside perimeter of the ring; inner boundary — the inside perimeter or front edge of viewers; and the inner space — that open space between the inner boundary and the collective focus. With the identification of these features comes the ability to analyze aspects of crowd behavior that were never before available or "seen." Milgram and Toch pursue this task by examining such form-relevant questions as the "permeability" of boundaries and the various implications for a crowd of having a defined shape with clearly marked boundaries, etc.

There are differences between their beginning statement and that which is developed from my empirical findings. For example, my observational data indicates that the "ring" is not the "natural" shape of crowds, per se, but that crowd shape is related to crowd function. Therefore, the "ring" is a shape that is particular to "viewing" a single focus under certain conditions. Furthermore, their discussion of crowd form is limited to the "ring." Other shapes and functions that crowds take and perform are not discussed.

With this small number of researchers ends our review of collective behavior theory and empirical findings. The demonstration of the importance of the nonverbal, both implicitly and explicitly, in prior works on crowds is complete. Now the more positive task of laying the ground work for the application of this understanding is at hand.

SECTION 3: FORM — THE RELEVANCE OF THE CONCEPT

This last section shifts our attention directly to the concept — form. The objective is twofold. First, it is to relate selected empirical findings and theoretical issues about the generic concept to an understanding of group form in collective behavior. Then the uses of the concept form in nonsociological literatures is indexed to the appropriate chapters where similar or related use is made.

For the reader who questions whether a collectivity of objects takes on a form or whether people impute forms to a collectivity of objects, attention is directed to Leonard Zusne's book, *Visual Perception of Form*.[63] It contains a bibliography of over 2,700 separate works: discussing, using, or measuring how man interacts with his environment in different ways involving form perception/projection. From this massive summary of psychological research and theory presented by Zusne, a few crowd-relevant findings are reported here.

First is the fact that people constantly (and necessarily) reduce the amount of sense data in their visual worlds by form identification.[64] Conversations between students of collective behavior are laced with such words as crowd, collective assembly, group. These all refer to a level of perceiving social phenomena that calls for the observer to ignore individuals and to attend to some quality that belongs to them as a collectivity. Such concepts as "in a line," "in a column," "in a marching formation," refer to one of these qualities manifested by a group, i.e., its form or shape.

Secondly, a multitude of research studies indicate that form recognition can be based on an amazing number of different qualities of individual elements and/or the relations between the individual elements. Color, shape and outline, spatial distances between elements, goodness of shape, complexity of shape, homogeneity of elements, orientation of elements to one another, symmetry of shape, are just a few of the "objective" features by which form comes to be recognized or imputed. Other factors that are more subjective or cultural in nature have also been found to be relevant, i.e., meaningfulness of the form, familiarity with the form, interest in a form, etc.[65]

The extension of these findings to collective behavior has problematic implications to the field researcher. Attempts to be rigorous or to designate the attributes in a crowd situation that members are using "to make" and "to see" forms are doomed to be only partially successful. The great number of independent and interacting factors that are present for form recognition, leaves the researcher with no recourse but to report on only the most seemingly germane of these features in a situation. In my descriptions and analysis of crowds, certain spatial behaviors are commonly related and identified as being those "things" in a situation that seem to be the elements out of which forms are most likely being created.

Zusne also reports that the total configuration of the form is determinable or recognizable from the viewing of only a segment of the whole. Within limits, this holds true even if the form is relatively complex or of diffused shape.[66] This is particularly important for understanding the dynamics of form recognition in crowds. The process of "seeing" the shape or form of the crowd often proceeds from a viewing of a piece of the whole. This is then understood, recognized, generalized, or associated with being a part of a total configuration without ever seeing the overall configuration. This imagined or projected "whole" provides a context of interpretation out of which meaning is given to the visible part. For example, one enters into a parade situation but only "sees" a small segment of the crowd's total formation. Yet, the segment visible to one's self is understood, and assigned a meaning in terms of an understanding that it is a part of an overall parade configuration.

I suggest that the individual's inability to see the total form of a crowd, either because of his location within it or to it or because the size of the formation prevents a ground level overview, does not negate the importance of form for the structuring of understanding the situation and the guidance of actions.

While psychologists have been busy establishing the whys and hows of the perception of form, other disciplines have also dealt with the question of form. Frank Lloyd Wright[67] developed a philosophy of architectural design centered around a relationship of form to function.

Adherents of this orientation hold that the form of any structure should be compatible with and follow the functions and activities within it. When actions are forced to artificially fit within a structure, form stands in conflict with function. This interferes with the very function the particular form was designed to encompass and may in fact inhibit the group function.

Chapters 2, 3, and 4 of this book address the group form-function relationship in collective behavior. Chapters 2 and 3 detail the manners in which group function determines group form. Chapter 4 reverses this question and shows how a group's form in turn affects the group function. It should be noted that the interactional/functional orientation as used does not attempt to make simple unidirectional, causal statements.

Geographers and urban sociologists are also concerned with the ecological consequences of the relationship of form to function. For example, in geography, much debate has been generated over what shape a central market area should have to be most functional. Urban sociologists, since the time of Park and Burgess, have frequently conceptualized the distribution pattern of certain social characteristics which occur in an urban area as taking on a special form (of concentric circles, sectors, etc.) as a consequence of certain social functions. Chapter 2 has an extended discussion as to the role of ecological factors in the form-function relation in collective behavior.

Through the efforts of one man, form in the study of communication, has practically become a household topic. Marshall McLuhan[68] has written several books stressing variations of his theme: the medium is the message, i.e., form communicates as much as content:

> . . . and we can now say, 'the medium is the message' quite naturally. Before the electric speed and total field, it was not obvious that the medium is the message. The message, it seemed, was the "content" as people used to ask what a painting was about. Yet, they never thought to ask what a melody was about, or what a house or a dress was about. In such matters, people retain some sense of the whole pattern, of form and function as a unity.[69]

While McLuhan has elaborated on how form communicates, ethologists have based much of their interpretations of animal behavior on the implicit assumption that forms do communicate. For example, the fact that red deer gather at a certain time of the year into a "herd" form, i.e., into a spatial proximity that is seen as a herd-form, is treated as communication via form. Depending upon the particular collective form that the deer adopt, different functions are held to be readable. Thus stags gathering together separate clusters of does is read as a mating form, while the gathering together of all the animals in a large linear form is read as a migratory pattern.[70]

Each of the chapters of this book deals with some aspect of the communicative function of group form. Chapter 5 is totally devoted to form and communication. It also contains analyses specifically on nonverbal communication and phenomenological factors in form recognition.

NOTES

1. Two-way radio communication between employees of Bureau of Land Management during the hour before "Evil Knievel" was to attempt to sky cycle across the Snake River Canyon, Twin Falls, Idaho. (Sam Wright field notes, 1974).

2. Ralph H. Turner and Lewis M. Killian, Collective Behavior, 2nd ed. (Englewood Cliffs, NJ: Prentice-Hall, 1972).

3. Ibid., p. 5.

4. Ibid., pp. 12-24.

5. Gustave Le Bon, The Crowd (New York: Ballantine Books, Inc., 1969).

6. Ibid., Chapter 1.

7. Ibid., p. 27.

8. Ibid., p. 127.

9. Ibid., pp. 31-32.

10. Ibid., p. 126.

11. Edward A. Ross, Foundations of Sociology, 2nd ed. (New York: The Macmillan Co., 1905). William McDougall, The Group Mind (New York: G.P. Putnam and Sons, 1920). Robert E. Park and Ernest Burgess, Introduction to the Science of Sociology (Chicago: University of Chicago Press, 1921).

12. See Chapter 5 for further elaboration of this point.

13. Herbert Blumer, "Collective Behavior," in New Outline of the Principles of Sociology, ed. C. Lee (New York: Barnes and Noble, 1951).

14. Carl Couch, "Dimensions of Association in Collective Behavior Episodes," Sociometry, 33 (1970), p. 463.

15. Blumer (1951), p. 170.

16. Ibid., p. 170.

17. Couch (1970), p. 469.

18. Ibid., p. 468.

19. Ibid., p. 465.

20. Ibid., p. 463.

21. Ibid., p. 462.

22. Ibid., p. 460.

23. Sigmund Freud, Group Psychology and the Analysis of the Ego (London: Hogarth Press, 1922).

24. Ibid., p. 21.

25. Ibid., p. 49.

26. Floyd H. Allport, *Social Psychology* (Boston: Houghton-Mifflin Co., 1924).

27. Ibid., p. 292.

28. Ibid., p. 312.

29. Neil E. Miller and John Dollard, *Social Learning and Imitation* (New Haven: Yale University Press, 1941).

30. Neil Smelser, *Theory of Collective Behavior* (New York: The Free Press, 1963).

31. Ibid., p. 152.

32. Daniel Katz, "The Psychology of the Crowd," in *Fields of Psychology*, ed. J.P. Guilford (New York: D. van Nostrand, 1940), pp. 145-162.

33. Alexander Mintz, "Non-adaptive Group Behavior," *Journal of Abnormal and Social Psychology*, 46 (1951), pp. 150-159.

34. Roger W. Brown, "Mass Phenomena," in *Handbook of Social Psychology Vol. II*, ed. G. Lindzey, (Reading, Mass: Addison Wesley, 1954) p. 842.

35. Richard A. Berk, "A Gaming Approach to Collective Behavior," *American Sociological Review*, 39 (1974), pp. 355-373.

36. Ralph H. Turner and Lewis M. Killian, *Collective Behavior* (Englewood Cliffs, N.J.: Prentice-Hall, 1957).

37. Ralph H. Turner, "Collective Behavior," in *Handbook of Modern Sociology*, ed. R. Fairs (Chicago: Rand McNally, 1964).

38. Turner and Killian (1972).

39. Ibid., p. 4.

40. Ibid., p. 22.

41. Ibid., p. 20.

42. Governor Shirley, "A Personal Correspondence, December 1, 1747," in *American Violence*, ed. Richard Hofstadter and Michael Wallace (New York: Random House, 1971), p. 61.

43. Turner and Killian (1972), p. 104.

44. Ibid., p. 38.

45. Antiwar Protestor/Police confrontation at the Federal Building, Sam Wright field notes; Los Angeles, California (May 11, 1972).

46. Charles Fisher, "Observing a Crowd: The Structure and Description of Protest Demonstrations," in *Research on Deviance*, ed. J.D. Douglas (New York: Random House, 1972).

47. Ibid., p. 207.

48. Ibid., p. 197.

49. Ibid., p. 195.

50. Clark McPhail, "Some Theoretical and Methodological Strategies for the Study of Crowd Phenomena," unpublished paper, 1972.

51. Brown, (1954) p. 839.

52. Ibid., p. 8.

53. Ibid., p. 9.

54. Margaret Stark, et. al., "Some Empirical Patterns in a Riot Process," *American Sociological Review*, 39 (1974, Dec.), pp. 865-876.

55. Carl Couch, "Dimensions of Association in Collective Behavior Episodes, " p. 459.

56. Ibid., pp. 459-460.

57. Ibid., p. 462.

58. Ibid., p. 461.

59. Berk, "A Gaming Approach to Collective Behavior" (1974) p. 366.

60. Ibid., p. 367.

61. Stanley Milgram and Hans Toch, "Collective Behavior: Crowds and Social Movements," in *Handbook of Social Psychology,* ed. G. Lindzey and E. Aronson, IV (Reading, Mass.: Addison Wesley, 1969), pp. 507-610.

62. Ibid., p. 518.

63. Leonard Zusne, *Visual Perception of Form* (New York: Academic Press, 1970).

64. Ibid., Chapters 2, 3, and 4.

65. Ibid., pp. 259-288.

66. Ibid., pp. 247-294.

67. Robert Sommer, *Personal Space: The Behavioral Basis of Design* (Englewood Cliffs, NJ: Prentice-Hall, 1969), p. 3.

68. Marshall McLuhan, *Understanding Media* (New York: Signet Books, 1964).

69. Ibid., p. 28.

70. William Etkin, *Social Behavior from Fish to Man* (Chicago: The University of Chicago Press, 1964), p. 17.

CHAPTER 2

HOW TASK FUNCTION DETERMINES GROUP FORM

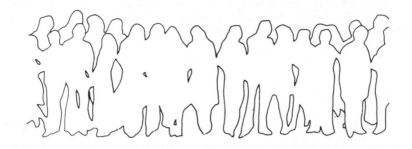

INTRODUCTION

Terms we normally employ to categorize an event of collective behavior, — riots, protests, parades — conceal more than they describe or explain behavior. What behaviors, mood states, symbolic displays, collective interactions are we able to say occurred when we are told that a riot took place? What do we know about the group nature of the event? What were the processes that characterized these interactions over time? What stages or phases of interaction were gone through? What were the participants' orientations to the event?

Any identifiable empirical referent to the term is further clouded by its political use. While police and politicians may describe a reference of behavior as a riot, those engaged in these behaviors may talk of a demonstration. At least in terms of "official" definitions, power and not "empirical fact," is the prime element in labeling. The lack of a specified behavior-concept relationship for most collective behavior terms makes conceptual abuse common place and rational under-standing of the phenomena difficult indeed!

What follows attempts to avoid and correct some of the above problems. By keeping the analysis grounded to the empirical, political and armchair characterizations are kept to a minimum. Conceptual distinctions made are likewise defined and discussed in terms of specified behaviors. Patterns, sequences, careers and processes that are said to describe collective behavior interactions have been derived inductively from observations, observations made of activities as they occurred in their natural settings.

The object of this chapter is to examine how the *"task" activities* engaged in by members of a collective assembly determine the *distribution of those members in space.* The configuration of the distribution of members in space, we have already labeled the "group form." This is an empirically (visually) available spatial pattern or shape that subgroups and groups have or take in the carrying out of collective activities. In part, this chapter offers instructions on how to see and to read these forms. There are two types of group forms — depending upon the activities which produce them. These are called **task forms** and **crowd forms**. Task forms are produced out of task activities. Crowd forms result from crowd activities.

a. *Task activities* — are the activities that members engage in which are particular to the goals, problems, of the occasion of collective assembly, e.g., parading, looting.

b. *Crowd activities* — are the recurring activities which members engage in that are universal to the recurrent goals, problems, of being in any situation of collective assembly, e.g., milling, converging.

Either task or crowd activities are present during all phases of collective assembly. More than this, all phases of collective activities that occur can be basically classified as being one type or the other. In effect, collective assemblies are understandable as such in terms of the continual emergence of task or crowd activities.

What we shall be considering in this and the following chapter are the group forms that are the products of task and crowd activities. To the extent that these activities are essential to the existence and maintenance of a task or of a crowd, they are functional to them. Therefore, we shall be examining the relationship between form and function, or more specifically, how function determines form.

This chapter analyzes task forms. It deals with such questions as: How do forms emerge out of the individual to individual spatial relations involved in the carrying out of a task? and How does a career of task forms appear over time as members advance through stages of task accomplishment? The next chapter carries on the analysis with a discussion of crowd forms and activities. Interaction between crowd activities and task activities is therein addressed.

THE BASIS OF TASK-FUNCTION AND GROUP FORM RELATION

We shall begin our analysis with a very selective descriptive account of the 1974 Rose Parade. It is selective in that what is reported here are only the observations from my notes that pertain to how people's individual-to-individual spatial relations give rise to group forms. And how structured spatial relationships emerge between these forms.

The account below is a verbal photograph. For the most part, it captures and freezes in place, for one moment, the general spatial distribution of people at a parade. It will provide the basis for our analysis of the relationship of task activities to task forms.

DESCRIPTIVE ACCOUNT # 1: A PARADE[1]

The floats of the Rose Parade passed by interspersed with marching bands, horses and rider groups, clowns, and cars of colorful entries. Both sides of the street, for miles, were lined with viewers. Those closest to the parade, either on the curb or within a couple of feet of the curb into the street, were, for the most part, sitting on the ground or in lawn-type chairs brought for the occasion. Immediately behind these were the standees. They were three to seven people deep, taking up the space between the curb and the sidewalk behind them.

The sidewalk was a constant jam of moving people. It was a river with two streams of bodies going in opposite directions with eddies and obstructions created by stopped people in midstream conversing, looking tired, etc. Teenagers were over-represented, on the sidewalk, but this was apparent only upon close inspection.

Bleachers filled with even more people flanked the sidewalks. They were set up on any space that would accommodate them — no matter how small. Behind the bleachers was another viewing fringe. Resident and apartment building windows, balconies, and roof tops were filled with spectators. These viewers were conspicuously enjoying cold beer and hot meals — fringe benefits of their location.

Radiating out from the parade route were other streams of people. Depending on the stage of the parade, these could be called arrivers and departees. Regardless of the time, there were always definite patterns of people who were moving into and out of the area.

Completing this picture is one last pattern.[2] Widely dispersed behind the scene are standing clusters of talking people. These are usually groups of from two to eight who are mostly engaged in loosely focused interaction with each other and the environment. These groups are dispersed from the area immediately behind the parade, back as far as a mile away from the parade itself.

From this account, two task activities are ascertainable as being essential to the makeup of the parade. These are audience activities and parading activities. Audience activities include such behavior as lining up along the parade route, moving about to find better places from which to see, and running parallel with some segment of the parade of special interest.

To understand the relationship between each task and its own form and the relationship between the tasks and forms to one another, requires beginning with individual relationships.

ELEMENTAL INDIVIDUAL SPATIAL ORIENTATIONS: AUDIENCE

Individuals, collectively performing an activity, stand in spatial orientation toward one another in a manner that is peculiar to the practical requirements of the activities. It is from individuals engaging in interactive activities necessary for the accomplishment of a task, that all else follows. For example, being a successful audience member in the parade situation, meant placing one's self in orientation to others so that you were: (1) stationary, (2) shoulder to shoulder, (3) facing in the same direction as the other audience members. Both the major types of members — the sitters and the standers — shared this orientation.

Furthermore, there was, of necessity, a fourth orientation, i.e., (4) face-to-back relations. These came out of the piling[3] of people one behind the other, as space immediate to the parade route became filled. As a consequence, the next layer of space would become occupied and so on, until a mass of people had "formed." This piling was irregular in all places, except the grandstands, where uniform front to rear relations existed as an artifact of the fixed seating arrangement. Piling also produced a fifth orientation in that (5) it placed most of the viewers in a surrounded position vis-à-vis one another. As a consequence, those in the middle are surrounded by others and hindered from readily moving about. Here, we see that one of the important effects of this collective activity is that densely-spaced bodies become a temporarily emergent feature of the physical environment.

a. Shoulder to
shoulder viewing

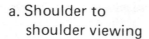
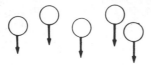

c. Grandstand

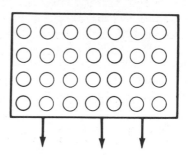

b. Piling

Figure 2.1   **Elemental spatial relationships of audience members in the parade situation**

THE RELATION OF TASK AND FORM: AUDIENCE

As individuals negotiate audience space and relations, an overall configuration begins to emerge. The resulting collective patterns of individuals in their audience orientations is thereby determined by the task of viewing, trying to view, etc.

The configurational form of the audience was a stationary, linear massing of individuals facing inwards to the parade route. Aerial photographs revealed two walls of bodies ten to fifteen feet thick, lining the route, with rectangular patches of bleachers filled with audience members behind these walls at staggered intervals. In short, the linear stationary wall form emerged out of the task activities of the audience members. The requirement of carrying out activities distributes members in space in a formational manner, characteristics of and recognizable as, the form peculiar to that task, i.e., viewing a parade.

ELEMENTAL INDIVIDUAL SPATIAL ORIENTATIONS: PARADING

In situations where the primary tasks are interdependent (e.g., parades) so are their spatial relations. Given that the task of the audience is to observe what the paraders are displaying, then the form of the parade activities interactionally influence the distribution of the audience. It is the parader's manner of being spatially distributed that is a major aspect of the practical task problem encountered in viewing.

These two activities are dependent upon one another for their existence. Without people presenting something to view, the audience would be unable to do viewing. Without the audience, those presenting something to be viewed, would not be presenting, i.e,. the parade had a twofold interdependent division of labor.

The overall formation of paraders emerging is that of: (1) moving clusters of people (separated from one another by open spaces of from ten to several hundred feet), (2) who are creating, occupying, and moving down a route, (3) filling the length of the path of the route with these clusters of people standing in a follow-the-leader, one behind the other, linear formation (separated on each side by a space from the audience).

a. INDIVIDUALS IN A UNIT

Military precesion

Clowns

b. UNITS

Band   Clowns   Mounted units

Figure 2.2 Individual spatial relationships of paraders

Let us turn to the examination of the parade activities and their forms so that the interaction between the two tasks can be dealt with further.

As with the audience, the paraders stand in individual spatial orientations to one another, as determined by the coordinated, joint task activities in which they are engaged. These individual relations are characterized by: (1) people moving, (2) in the same direction, (3) in and along the same route, (4) usually from a starting point "a" to a termination point "b." (The movement can be in step and on line, but whether or not there is military precision, individuals are moving in relation to one another in a general), (5) shoulder to shoulder, and (6) patterned face-to-back relationship.

THE RELATION TO TASK AND FORM: PARADERS

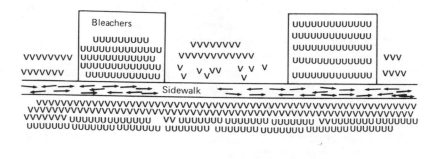

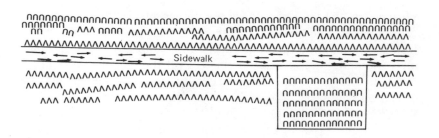

Figure 2.3 Audience form
Key to standard symbols used in all figures: **U** sitting; **V** standing; milling.

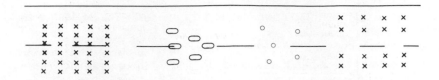

Figure 2.4 Parader form

To accomplish the task of putting on parade something to be viewed, paraders actually become concerned with a portion of the configurational display that emerges from their individual relationships, i.e., how their group looks. Groups of individuals can pass by spelling out words with their body orientations or in formations of military precision — in step, on line, multi-linear — uniformity produced from the simultaneous coordination of body orientations and movement. The concern with group formation appearance is also accompanied by a concern with subgroup boundary maintenance. Thus, groups of individuals move down the parade route in spatially separated clusters, e.g., a marching band separates itself from the units in front and back of it and from the audience on the sides. The importance of boundary maintenance in a formal parade is emphasized by the assignment of outriders whose responsibility is to maintain these distances and to curb the daring demeanor of kids who violate these boundaries by dashing across the street.

THE PARADE FORM: A PRODUCT
OF ITS TWO FUNCTIONS

From this, the total parade form emerges. It appears as a spatial corridor whose walls are made of the audience, between which move clusters of spatially separated paraders following one another in a single file pattern. The passing clusters fill the corridor, depending upon their width, to within three to twenty feet of the audience. (The parader-audience collective orientation is side to face with the viewers facing the sides of the paraders' formation.) To sum up, there are two main functional tasks, or a twofold task division of labor in the parade situation. Different activities are required of members carrying out one or the other of the tasks. The activities of each task result in the members assuming task-determined spatial orientations towards one

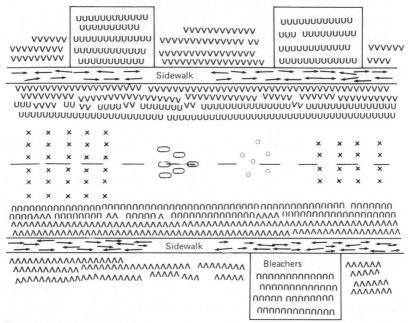

Figure 2.5 Parade form

another. Emerging from these individual spatial relations is a larger spatial form of the task being performed — e.g., the viewer-parader spatial form. From the spatial interrelationship between the two tasks, an overall form emerges that is characteristic of the parade in general.

SOME GENERAL COMMENTS ON FORM ANALYSIS

An examination of a group's form as an interactional product always requires going through the above steps. That is, an examination of first the elemental spatial orientations and then the task forms that emerge. In those situations, where two or more task groups are in interaction, there must be an examination of the interactions between the task forms to understand how the emergent base of the total form appears.

Audience-performer relation is a general type of which the parade is one possible kind. The general type has the same basic type of relations as the parade, the difference being that each subtype has its own peculiar task problems (e.g., stationary presenters on a stage rather than the moving presenters of a parade) which, in turn, determine the formational relations.

As we shall see, not all collective activities involve more than one task. In not all situations where more than one task is being carried out are these tasks interactionally interdependent. Nor in all situations, with more than one group interacting with one another, do they do so with one group automatically dominating the spatial interactions.

ENVIRONMENT — FORM RELATIONS

Before going further, the question of environment or ecological influence on crowds shape versus task-form relation can be addressed.

With one exception, no authors writing on collective behavior have tried to integrate spatial factors involved in crowd relations into a general discussion on crowd behavior. Instead, crowd shape and member distribution in space is treated mainly as a dependent variable of a physical setting. The claim being made here is not that environment (the ecological setting) has no effect on crowd shape. What is argued is that task relations have an independent and determinant effect on members' distribution, which environment influences. Changing environmental factors may change objective conditions from parade situation to parade situation. These changes in environment become interactional problem-conditions that paraders and audiences must deal with at each parade, but the parade form itself will appear over and over again, in each environmental setting. The question then becomes:

> How does the environment influence the necessary spatial relations that members must take to one another in the carrying out of task activities, if the task is to become accomplished?

The first influence is a totally negative one. As Smelser[4] indicates, environment can prevent a task from being performed altogether by not providing the space necessary for the task's implementation. For example, if people need to assemble collectively in one setting, and no space exists for this, then the absence of the spatial area necessary for the task prevents the task from occurring.

In large, modern, urban areas, the political control of appropriate spaces for collective assembly can be used to prevent the assemblies from occurring. During the early years of the U.S. involvement in Vietnam, many Park Commissions consistently denied permits for antiwar rallies in these public domains. Likewise, police frequently withheld parade permits for antiwar marches.

As a consequence, much antiwar effort, in these years, was aimed at obtaining legal permission for assembling in those areas having appropriate shape and space for supporting group forms that would emerge as an effect of the task activities — large circumference park areas for rallies and narrow, but long, street areas for a marching form. By politically blocking these areas, officials forced antiwar protesters into a physical environment that would not support the group form of these activities.

The second influence the environment can have on task function and so on the task formation, is by affecting how the task is carried out. That is, the environment becomes a part of the practical problems of task activities. Turner and Killian note that communication necessary for successful accomplishment of a task can be interfered with by the environment.[5] This is one of the important ways that environment becomes an interactional problem in task activities, as exemplified below.

DESCRIPTIVE ACCOUNT #2: A SIT-IN[6]

The stated goal was to occupy the University's Administration building until the Chancellor met the demands for a minority program. The 800 plus of us had only been in the building ten minutes when the rumor circulated that the leaders had reached an agreement with the Chancellor. When a skinny fellow in a Levi shirt loudly voiced this fact, a cheer went up from us in this area of the first floor. As the word spread, this was followed by a series of cheers from the other areas of the first floor. There was then a general rush to leave the building as the group cohesion broke down and people turned from their group orientation to private matters. This seemed to require leaving first or the fastest so the building emptied out with a rapid and cheerful pandemonium.
(Notes taken outside)

There is something wrong. There do not seem to be as many people diverging from the area as had entered it. Perplexed . . . I am waiting by the tree at the Northwest corner of the building.

Two minutes have passed . . . I guess I was wrong, everyone seems to have left.

I am going to go back inside and pick up on how the secretarial/administrative staff reacted to this latest invasion.

. . . Ha! . . . Unbelievable . . . Just discovered why not as many people had left as had entered. The second floor, where the Chancellor's office is located, is still being occupied. The rumor that the first floor occupants had acted in terms of was wrong! So the sit-in reality is still in effect up here while the bottom floor has long since been emptied . . . Incredible!

The physical structure of the building had led to a communication gap between those on different floors. However, the effect of environment on communication is not constant.

Environment influences task communication and so members' spatial distribution, only in terms of the specific communication needs of members pursuing a certain kind of task. Different collective tasks enacted in the same environment will experience the environmental influence on communication differently, according to the specific needs of the task.

Later that week a march through the administration building was planned and carried out without any hitches. This task activity required people to simply follow those in front of them. This minimized leader-follower communication needs in the same environment that before, when a different task was involved, had been a hindrance.

Again, we see that the environment affects the spatial distribution of members in terms of their task activities, and not directly.

Finally, environment can influence task activities by changing in the middle of the activities. Thus, a fire in a theater is a change in the environment that negates spatial conditions necessary for the task of movie watching. Any further influence of the environment on the members' spatial distribution depends on what task activities the members try to engage in whether to fight the the fire, to flee, or to pray.

THE SPATIAL CAREER OF A TASK

To this point, the primary aim has been to elaborate on the nature of the task-form relationship. It must be emphasized that a static description is not adequate for understanding these relationships.

Interactional relations are continually unfolding in negotiation. Therefore, no matter how detailed in description and insightful a static account might be, it captures only one moment in the dynamics of changing interaction.

The parade-audience activities had a career of changing spatial relations. The parade scene described came in the middle of the carrying out of the task. It, therefore, missed other spatial relations that appeared during the history of the parade — e.g., many people were in the streets prior to the parade's beginning and would pour back into the streets after the parade. During the parade there would be gaps in clusters of paraders, such that the collective focus of the audience would break down and one-to-one interactions would appear until the next group came along. That is to say, different problems are encountered in the accomplishing of tasks over a period of time. Individuals dealing with the different problems in carrying out a task place themselves in changing spatial orientation to one another as they continually adjust to continual, situational change.

The account below will offer us the opportunity of examining looting as an activity that requires changing spatial relations to be fully carried out. From this description, ideal typical phases of the career of looting will be constructed using task-form analysis. Generalization from this specific kind of collective assembly to collective assembly as a generic type can then be made.

DESCRIPTIVE ACCOUNT #3: LOOTING IN THE WATTS RIOT[7]

. . . As I was making a right turn on the street where the action was centered, several Negro youths ran up to my car. They said, "Turn your inside lights on, Blood, so we can see who it is.

. . . . Large numbers of men, women and children were gathered on both sides of the street with bricks and other objects in their hands. Just up the street was a car which had been upturned and set afire.

. . . A car came roaring down the street. The crowd yelled: "Whitey! Get him!"

. . . Bricks, stones and pipes, hurled from both sides of the street, dented both sides of the car. The front windshield was smashed. The car speeded up and kept going until it was out of the area.

. . . The people around, watching the man being beaten, kept yelling: "Beat the _____ _____. Teach him to keep his ass out of Watts."

The behaviors described so far have significant bearing on several of the theories and issues discussed in Chapter 1. We see that, despite individual states of emotional arousal, individual interpretive behavior is being routinely carried out. Judgements are being made as to what and who are the symbolic objects of hostility, i.e., "Whitey." Furthermore in the midst of these activities instructions are given to a "Blood" as to how to avoid the dangers of a mistaken identity, i.e., "Turn your inside lights on" and, in effect, what the emergent norms are. The irrational behavior assumptions of contagion/imitation theories must be evaluated in terms of this seemingly "contextually" or "situationally rational" behavior or — preferably — interpretive behavior.

Likewise, Freudian statements that crowds act the way they do because of leadership-follower love frustration, are inconsistent with these empirical facts. The total absence of symbolic leaders prevails in every situation herein described. This is quite consistent with the findings of the previously mentioned study by Stark, et al., that the riot itself literally encompassed many square miles of people. A fact difficult to reconcile with an assumption of follow-the-leader, as the readers can judge for themselves in the continuing account.

A brick came out of nowhere and smashed through the window of a hot dog stand across the street.

Someone yelled: "That's Whitey's, tear it down." A number of people from both sides of the street converged on the stand and began breaking all the windows. Several men climbed into this stand and began passing out cokes and other beverages to the people outside.

After they had completey depleted the stock of wines, cokes and everything else of value that could be carried out, they evacuated the stand and began walking down the street toward a couple of stores. They did not set fire to this stand.

. . . A liquor store and grocery store were the next targets. First, the windows were knocked out. Then the people poured into the stores — men, women, children. They rushed back and forth, in and out, carrying as much as they could: groceries, liquor and cigarettes.

Two police cars came roaring down the street and pulled up in front of the store. The people inside came rushing out and ran right by the policemen who made no attempt to stop or apprehend them. The police got out of their cars and set up a temporary blockade in front of the store with their rifles pointed toward the crowd across the street. They remained there for approximately fifteen minutes and left. Before they had gotten a half block away, the looting resumed.

Next door to the liquor store was a meat market. These windows also were smashed and people in cars drove up and began loading meat into the trunks of their cars. Two young boys (they looked to be nine or ten years old) came running out of the store and across the street carrying a side of beef. The crowd roared its approval and greeted the boys with laughter and cheers.

Several men came walking toward me laden down with liquor. One of them paused in front of me and asked: "What do you drink, Brother?" He and the others stopped right there in the street to have a drink.

. . . The people piled into cars and headed for 103rd Street. Others followed on foot.

. . . When we reached the main street . . . a few hundred people had already arrived.

. . . The iron gratings in front of the stores and businesses were forced first. Then the windows broken. Dozens of people climbed in and out of the stores with armloads of clothing, appliances, guns and liquor.

The next two paragraphs of this account, and the already described liquor store looting, are of great importance. They directly challenge a major assumption of many collective behavior theorists and of a dominant school of sociological thought — that collective behavior equals social disorganization, and, stemming from this, that police are restoring social order when they seek to control such behavior.

It is clear that from the position of the members of the collectivity, police are the cause of the disruption of the on-going social order. The disorganization by the police of the task activities of looting is, in these two instances, socially restored to its natural equilibrium state upon the departure of the police. Social disorganization, as used by Le Bon and others, is a political term not an empirically based analytic term.

Coordinated task activities, i.e., social organizations, are the basic structural reality of collective behavior. It is for this reason that we have proceeded from a description of the task activities of the legitimate formal collective organization of the parade to this riot activity. The task (function) – form analysis of the riot to follow, will be of an "illegitimate," informal, shifting, emergent, but nevertheless, real collective organization of behavior.

There were three squad cars that went back and forth on 103rd street. The policemen made no attempt to get out of them and stop the looting. However, the people would run out of the stores just as the police cars approached the business area and hide in the alleys or behind the stores.

As soon as the cars had passed the looting would continue. Walking back and forth on both sides of the street, I paused at a pawnshop and observed several people coming out with portable TVs, record players, sewing machines and clothes.

. . . A very young Negro boy was picking up a case of cuff links someone had dropped. A policeman roared: "Put that down." The boy quickly dropped the case and walked away.

. . . The officer replied: "Well, get off the street and stay off the street."

The woman stood very defiantly in front of them and made no move to go back inside the laundromat. The police looked menacingly at her and then at me. They turned and walked back to their cars.

Turning around, I saw approximately fourteen Negro people who had been inside the laundromat now standing in the doorway.
. . . There were large numbers of Negroes congregated on porches, in parked cars and just standing along the curb, even at this early hour of the morning.

The spatial relations available for reconstruction of this account have a complexity that is far different from those of the parade. As distinct from the parade, the activities in this situation are: (1) for the most part, emergent, i.e., not institutional, planned, anticipated or predictable; (2) frequently several tasks being simultaneously and independently pursued in the same area — looting, beating up of white people, rock throwing; (3) an interchange of members between tasks-activities; (4) activities which appear and disappear from the situation altogether as they are replaced by other ones; (5) looting, which does not require an audience, as does the parade, i.e., it is not interdependently related to other groups. In most instances there are viewers (police, TV cameramen, passersby) but these are not necessary to the carrying out of the task as is the audience by the parade.[8] Finally, (6), there is the already mentioned major difference in the type of knowledge available to us in this account, by virtue of what the observer has reported. That is, we can see in some detail the processes involved in carrying out each phase of the task activities over time.

From the details of the process of looting, a typified developmental career can be constructed. Phases of the career are delineated in terms of the changing interactional problems encountered in the carrying out of the task. According to our task-form thesis, different problematic activities place people in different individual spatial orientations, and so produce different collective spatial configurations. Therefore, we can expect to find that each phase has its own unique identifiable form.

PHASE I — FOCUSING

The initial change from one activity to another (e.g., from beating to looting) is frequently distinguished by a significant event or keynoting action. (The word "keynoting" or "significant" tend to be misleading in their implication of also being dramatic. That meaning is not intended here. By significant we mean to describe whatever factor is significant to a change. This could be boredom or the completion of another task. The term "phase" indicates that an interactional stage is gone through in which a certain kind of problem is accomplished that was necessary for the completion of a task.)

FIVE SPATIAL PHASES OF A TASK CAREER

In the "Hot Dog Stand" situation, a brick through the window, accompanied by the yell, "That's Whitey's, tear it down," ended the beating and become the first phase of the looting.

In this phase, members are spatially distributed and oriented to one another according to whatever task activities that they happen to have been engaged in at the time. The orientations to one another which indicate the beginning of a new and different type of task are that of common focusing. The collective switch of orientation from "whatever" to a common social object, at the very minimum, makes members (1) look-up and (2) look in the same direction orientation, towards the same object or focus.

The overall patterned appearance is that of people dispersed in an area — at spatial distances from one another that are not consistent with the present focus or attention attitudes displayed or rather they are consistent with a focus-activity disjunction. It is a pattern of

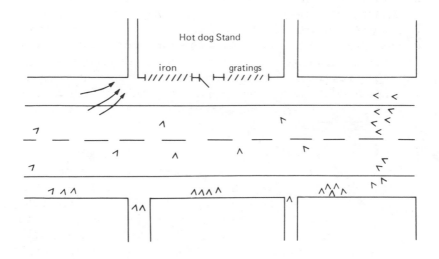

Figure 2.6 Focusing

people "looking up" from whatever they are doing while their body orientation is still consistent with that of their old activities. This configuration we shall call "focusing."

PHASE II — CONVERGENCE

All changes of activity require movement. This can vary from the slightest shifting of individual to individual orientations to one another, to the crossing of a space separating the future sites of activity from the present location of members.

When the hot dog stand ("A") became the general focus of the members' orientation, there was movement from various surrounding spatial positions toward point "A." Individual spatial orientations towards one another, therefore, became (1) facing a common direction, (2) moving across the open space, (3) shoulder to shoulder and face to back relations for those runnning at different rates from the same general area, and (4) a semicircle of closing relationships with those converging from other directions.

This phase has an overall pattern that is understandable only over time. Individuals moving collectively are observed in order to deter-

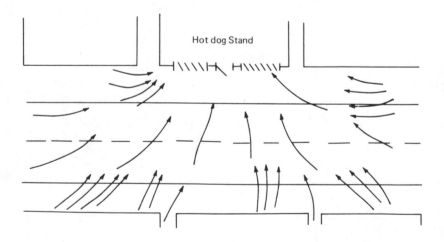

Hot dog Stand

Figure 2.7 Converging

mine their paths of movement. This requires at least two separate looks to fix direction and consistency of movement or one long look. This spatial configuration of converging paths of movement can be characterized as a *convergence.*

PHASE III — PERFORMING THE TASK

A. Invasion. Gaining entry to the place converged upon required some division of labor. This can involve the simple problem of those in front breaking a window or brushing away glass. In those instances where an iron grating barred entry, then even more cooperative efforts were required. Where a large number of people have converged, then: (1) a semicircle of shoulder to shoulder, (2) face to back, (3) stationary viewing relations will emerge around, (4) those directly

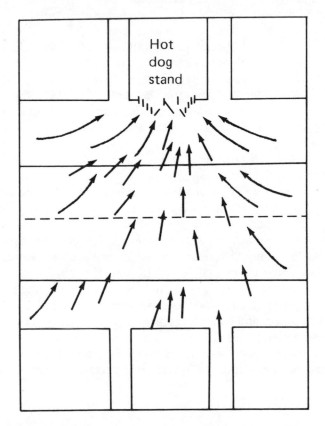

Figure 2.8 Invasion

engaged in breaking in. A work space between the viewers and the looters will most likely emerge. The actives will be oriented spatially to one another in a shifting choreography of coordinated-task specific behavior. People in this type of situation are in an invasion-viewer configuration.

B. Looting. The actual removal of goods from a premise, in one case, entailed a division of labor. Goods were passed from the inside to those on the outside. Other stores were physically constructed to allow free entry to all. In these cases, more individual parallel efforts were possible, i.e., every man for himself. In those instances, where large objects were taken (the side of meat), two or three people might cooperate in its removal.

Looting activity is primarily characterized by the spatial movement of goods by people out of a premise. Depending upon the circumstance, this can entail a division of labor or independent individual efforts, and bodily entering into the premise or simply reaching in through a broken window. Basic individual-to-individual orientations will be of two kinds: (1) those facing and moving inward in shoulder to shoulder, face to back relations, and (2) those in the same relationship but moving outward from the store or premise (with those moving out most likely to have goods in their hands while those moving in are empty handed).

The overall pattern would be two moving streams in and out of a premise, with each stream inter-penetrating the other. This can be called the *looting configuration.*

C. Interruption (Time-out Intermissions). During the course of the acts of breaking in, of looting or of termination, interruptions can occur which temporarily reorient people to the spatial situation. Police appearance and/or actions were responsible for hiding, fleeing and in one case, "dropping the goods." In the above account, return to the interrupted phase of the task action became the major response.

The spatial configurations particular to the interruption phase varied according to circumstance, the phase of the activity which is being interrupted, and individual variations in response. The behavior in the interrupted phase is visible as that spatial activity which exists during a period when another activity is stopped and then later reengaged in. The overall configuration appears as movement and can

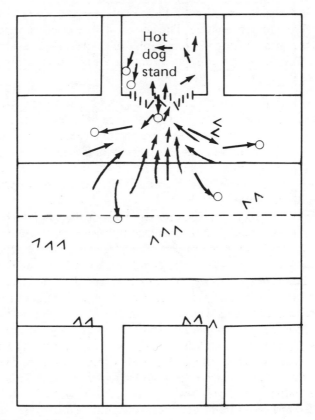

Figure 2.9 Looting

be designated as an engagement, disengagement, reengagement configuration of spatial movement, or *interruption configuration.*

PHASE IV — DIVERGENCE

There are several sets of individual-to-individual orientations involved in leaving the site of a looting incident. Those with large valuables and nonpocketable items tend to leave the scene altogether in order to secure the relocation and possession of the goods. Others appear to move together to the next site, sometimes participating more in the break-in than in the looting. While yet another type will consume and/or distribute recently looted goods, e.g., liquor. All the orientations eventually result in moving away from site "A" to other

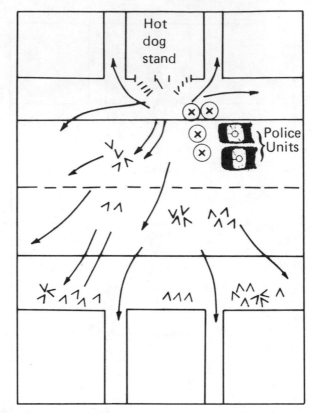

Figure 2.10 Interruption

locations. In general, this involves spatial orientations of: (1) backs turned away from the looted site, (2) movement toward other directions, (3) shoulder to shoulder, and (4) face to back irregular distributions of members over space.

There are three patterns of member distribution discernible here: those leaving the area altogether, those moving to the next site, and those standing about. The total form is of intermingling subpatterns i.e., *divergence*.

ANALYSIS

As the ongoing problems involved in carrying out activities of practical tasks change, so do the spatial distributions of members. A typology of the phases of the career of these activities has been

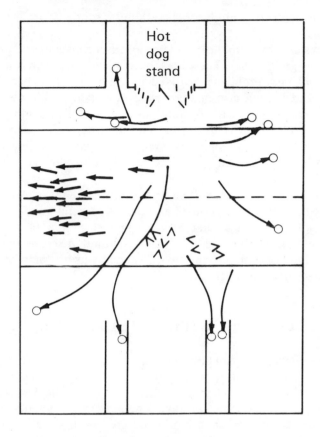

Figure 2.11 Divergence
Key to standard symbols used in all figures: ⊗ police;
→○ looters with loot.

constructed. The advantage of this classification scheme over others is its emphasis on the elemental spatial changes of interaction over time.

By using the spatial career approach, the referent of the term "looting" becomes understood to be a specifiable empirical interactional process unfolding over time. By analyzing the spatial descriptions of many looting events, common spatial careers will appear.

The ideal typical phases identified here for looting are (1) focusing, (2) converging, (3) tasks, (a) invasion, (b) looting, (c) interruption (time-out) (4) diverging. Similar interactional problems are involved in carrying out similar tasks of looting in different situations. These will place members in predictable and similar spatial forms in different situations.

Parades also have unique problems and as a consequence, uniquely identifiable group forms. These we looked at in detail when considering the special task problems involved in carrying out a parade. But parades and looting also share certain universal problems and, so, forms that are common to all situations of collective assembly. These are *converging, task,* and *diverging.* Furthermore, their career patterns are the same. That is, people converged to the parade setting, became engaged in the task, and upon task completion there was collective divergence.

In the next section, we will analyze an event that serially came to involve three different collective tasks. A careful reading of this account of the homosexual protest against police brutality and entrapment in Hollywood, California, should disclose the above career pattern of form presentation. Especially as this pattern repeats itself three times in succession.

A COLLECTIVITY WITH A MULTI-TASK CAREER

Some collectivities can be essentially characterized by their pursuit of one task. Their spatial career, and living history as an entity, ends with the accomplishment of the task, for example, the parade. Other situations are remarkable for having present many independent and simultaneously operating task-oriented groups. Individual members may confine themselves to one task or may move between groups within the setting, e.g., looting, stoning, burning, etc. These groups come and go, interchange members and shift focus with some frequency.

Other crowds are noticeable for their consistency of identity over time, while sequentially pursuing a series of different tasks and keeping the same members. The resulting crowd activities are characterizable by the sequential presentation of their task-related spatial careers. The following account, of a homesexual protest against police brutality, is of this nature.

DESCRIPTIVE ACCOUNT #4 — A HOMOSEXUAL PROTEST[9]

I arrived at the park at 10:00 a.m. This was an hour before the protest rally was to begin. Males, mostly in their twenties and early thirties, converged on the park over the next hour, from every direction. Approximately 60 percent were on foot while the rest arrived by car. The available parking spaces around the park were soon filled.

Prior to the rally, activity in the park was mostly of a milling and unfocused or noncollective task interaction. Groups of men in knots of two to eight stood about talking. Others, singly or in groups of twos, threes, and fours moved about. There was organizing activity going on in the last fifteen minutes prior to the beginning of the rally. This was manifested mainly in terms of equipment being set up, e.g., microphones, food tables, etc.

When the rally was brought into collective focus, toward the speakers' dias, a circling of this focus took place. Those in a 180 degree arc in front of the speaker, made up the main body of the 350+ men, present at that time. The forty or so men scattered in the 180 degree arc behind the speakers' dias were mostly those who had before been doing the preparing. (This special location of "in" group members in relation to the focus, is a repeated feature of almost all public meetings.) Several speakers harangued the crowd, but none as successfully as the Episcopal minister of the Homosexual Church. Where before there had been many aside conversations during talks, he literally received the undivided attention of all. When he announced that we should all take a placard and proceed to the Hollywood Police Station, three blocks away, there was an immediate response.

The circle of men broke down and the crowding in and around the signs took place. Those who got a sign would then join friends and the stream of men now moving down the sidewalk on both sides of the street. Early in this process someone yelled out, and it was greeted with widespread laughter, "Should we march or skip there?" Soon all were stretched out between the park and the station.

When I arrived at the station, two moving picketing circles of men had already emerged — one on each of the sidewalks in front of the station. Other arrivees would either join the picketers, or move about between the picketers and the audience of observers. A squad of riot dressed police stood "at ready" in a semicircle around the entrance of the building.

A point to be expanded on in the next chapter is worthy of a contextual comment here. Motivational imputation to audience members viewing the form of a collective activity is hazardous. Audience members are not necessarily the more passive or less involved bystanders. Often the opposite is the case. Volatile members who do not have the patience or interest in participating in "ordinary" collective activities, such as picketing, often constitute a sizable proportion of an audience. As the following reveals, the "Storm Troopers" learned this fact the hard way:

> This activity continued for ten minutes when eight men dressed in full Nazi uniform, with swastika arm band, approached from the direction of Sunset Boulevard. The chants, which before had been directed at the police, were now directed at these new symbolic objects. The Nazis were greeted with the repeated collective taunts of "Nazis are Queer, Nazis are Queer!"
>
> While the picketing circles continued unabated, with no loss of membership, the audience group, closest to the destination point of the Nazis' path, turned towards them. This rapidly developed into a confrontation situation which caused the Nazis to stop about ten feet from the facing audience.
>
> The Nazi leader began an interview with a T.V. newsman, but interrupted it when a crowd member loudly suggested that he "probably gave great blow-jobs." The enraged Nazi then closed the distance between themselves and the stationary taunters until they were face to face.
>
> It was hard to say who threw the first punch. Regardless, the confrontation turned quickly into an ignoble rout. The badly outnumbered and beaten Storm Troopers fled back up the street and incredibly, all was as before in less than two minutes. The audience members returned to their viewing activities.

The sounds enveloping many types and phases of collective behavior are cacaphonious. Hundreds of conversations going on at once, squeals of excitement, yells of challenge, shouts of anger and confrontation, organizers using megaphones, police with bull horns, and then there are the ever present chants. This particular protest used shouts not just to communicate messages about symbolic issues, "Gays are people too!", but also to taunt their enemies, "Nazis are Queer" and, as follows, as devices to "verbally" coordinate their collective activities:

> After an hour, the chant was begun, "we're going to go now, we're going to go now." The repeating of this was the occasion for many audience members to turn and go off into directions away from the park. The main body then proceeded to stream back to the park. There were approximately 100 fewer men than had set out. The last of the returnees

were not yet at the park when an instance of successful emergent leadership took place (the only one I have ever encountered before or since). The priest/leader was trying to reassemble the rally form, so that a concluding prayer could be given. A young man, in a group of fifteen other men, to the rear of the emergent rally form, was yelling out, "No, we're not done yet, let's go to Hollywood Blvd., after all, it belongs to us, doesn't it?"

The emergent leader did not take time to argue with the priest. He set off with his group of fifteen. This pulled the audience apart and created two separate foci. A few men who were in the main body began to run to catch up with those headed towards Hollywood Boulevard. They came to fill the space between the main body and the moving away insurgences. The overall effect was of a sizable spread. This was particularly so, because those who had simply been leaving to go home, in the direction of Hollywood Boulevard, became mixed in with the insurgents. The remaining 150 men looked to the priest for direction. When he finally decided to support the emergent move, the insurgents were a full block away. We walked quickly for the next four blocks, in the hot sun, before we overtook the first group, who had now stopped and were waiting for us.

When we finally all caught up, the original organizers reestablished control, put out marching monitors and declared a goal. We were to march down Hollywood Boulevard (on a Saturday, in the hot summer sun, in the middle of the tourist season, carrying placards with a half dozen messages, — "All cops are queer," "Out of the closet into the street" — through the heart of the business district). A quick head count revealed about 140 men in the marching formation. The march was to be on the sidewalk. Two police motorcycle officers appeared and cooperated with this illegal parade and stopped traffic for us at each intersection. This service was negotiated in exchange for our staying out of the street. By-standers' reactions to our appearance were mostly in the form of uncomprehending stares. Verbal comments were made mostly from the safety of cars. There were a balance of negative and positive ones. One sympathetic comment was, "Well, we all can't be truck drivers."

Before the march had reached Hollywood and Vine, much complaining began to take place. Besides the general repetition of "how physically exhausting" this all was (and indeed, it took all my resolve not to drop out for a cool drink in a bar). The most common complaints were the lack of meaning in the situation: "What are we doing?" "Where are we going?" "What is this all about?" "When is this going to end?"

The turn off Hollywood Boulevard towards the park was greeted with a cheer and a quickening of pace. When we reached the park our

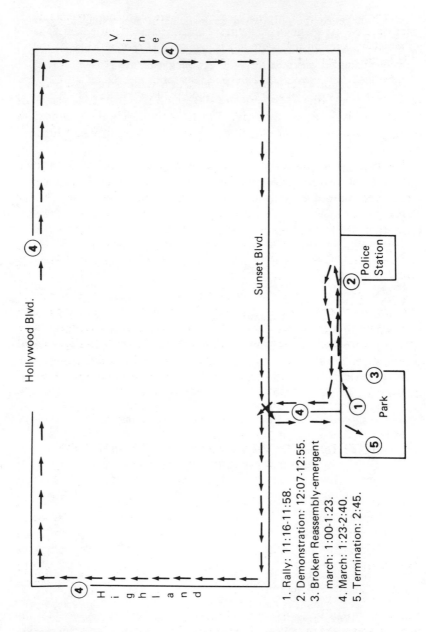

Figure 2.12 The homosexual protest

numbers were down to less than 80. There were no attempts to reassemble us. Within five minutes, I and a group of four prostrate ex-marchers were all that were left in the area as residual signs of the activities which had occurred over the last several hours.

In this account we can see how a collectivity of actors can become involved in carrying out a series of different tasks over time. Each of these tasks reflects the form peculiar to the problem encountered in doing the activity. But the sequence of forms temporally surrounding each task form was the same.

The men converged on the park. The thin linear streams of bodies coming from all directions became more pronounced as they began to merge near their destination. At the park an unfocused milling mass steadily grew. When the rally was started the audience-speaker formation quickly appeared. At the rally's termination there was a diverging from the park as two very dense streams moved down the sidewalks converging on the Hollywood Police Station. There a circulating picket formation took shape.

The breakdown of the picketing formation flowed into two diverging streams which converged at the park. There milling was brought into focus as an emergent march formation took shape. Men diverged away from the park and a block away set up a formal march configuration. They were soon joined by the other converging hold outs, and, thus, it continues — converging, task, diverging, converging, task, diverging, etc.

OUTLINE FORMAT FOR REPORTING ON COLLECTIVE BEHAVIOR

Inductively derived knowledge can be used as a basis for "giving empirical substance" to collective behavior concepts. Describing this "protest demonstration," as labeled by the press, first entails the identification of the collective tasks that occur, i.e., the rally, the demonstration, and the emergent march. Each task in turn should be broken down into its appropriate subpatterns, as was demonstrated with the looting incident. Then other forms should be noted, e.g., converging, milling, audience, diverging. The entire encounter can now be presented in temporal sequence. Below in outline format style is a summary report on the homosexual protest.

TASK I — THE RALLY: 10:00 TO 11:58

I — Converging movement from various points to park: 10:00 to 11:16. (convergence)

1. Converging movement from various points to park.

   a. By foot — from all directions, in groups of 1 to 5.
   b. By car — from all directions, in groups of 1 to 5.

2. Milling in Park — intermixed spatially. (milling)

   a. Groups of 1 to 8 — talking
   b. Groups of 1 to 4 — moving about
   c. Groups of 1 to 5 — organizing and setting up the equipment.

II — Rally stage: 11:16 to 11:58 a.m. (task)

1. Rally is focused (formed up with P.A. announcement)
   a. Aggregation of leaders at dias.
   b. Converging, closing in on dias — audience formation.
   c. Circle of bodies around dias — the largest number at the front, with a few members in the back.

2. Rally speakers speaking.

   a. Mixed collective focus and small group interactions.
   b. Unfocusing between speakers — much smaller group interaction.
   c. Refocusing to new speakers with — continuation of small group interaction.

3. Termination of Rally. (divergence)

   a. Last speaker gets undivided focus.
   b. Call to get picket signs — simultaneous movement and collapse of audience formation.

TASK II — THE DEMONSTRATION: 11:58 TO 12:55

I — The Migration from park to station: 11:58 to 12:07 (converging)

1. Movement from signs to sidewalks.
2. Movement from collapse rally to sidewalk.
3. Movement from both sides of sidewalk to station.
4. Some people in yard along the way — stationary and staring.

II— The Demonstration stages: 12:07 to 12:55 (task)

1. The forming-up stage.

   a. People begin forming and moving into picket lines.
   b. Others converge in audience clusters at street corners.
   c. Others mill about between the two.
   d. Police in semi-circle at entrance and atop local buildings.

2. The simultaneous protest and confrontation forms: 12:11 to 12:29. (Secondary task emerges)

    a. Audience members turn to approaching Nazis. (convergence)

    b. Converging Nazis stop ten feet from audience.

    c. Nazis close distance to audience and fight ensues. (task)

    d. Nazis flee a half block up the street and form into marching formation and march out of sight. (divergence)

    e. Audience returns to viewing.

III Termination of Protest and Migration from station to Park: 12:55 to 1:00 p.m. (divergence from protest site, convergence to park)

1. Chant about leaving — many audience members leave in other directions other than park.

2. Moving picketers begin to stream from police station towards park.

3. Audience and millers fall in behind the moving picketers.

TASK III — THE EMERGENT MARCH: 1:00 TO 2:40

I — The Broken Reassembly

1. The attempted reassembly form-up. 1:00 to 1:23

    a. Converging into and milling in park — much movement.

    b. The attempt for form-up of a focused reassembly —organizers at dias.

    c. The keynoting challenge and moving away of fifteen men.

    d. Two focuses, two groups with the insurgent group moving away.

2. The Emergent form of the march. (divergence from park)

    a. The dissenting members leave stationary group and move between the groups to catch up with the moving insurgent group.

    b. Comingling of insurgents with the new members in that direction for other reasons.

    c. The main body chooses to enjoin the insurgents and begins to move in that direction.

    d. The few members left behind in the park leave in other directions.

II —The March: 1:23 to 2:40

1. The form-up stage. (convergence)

    a. Insurgents stop and wait in aggregate group.

      b.   The trailing members trail in and join group.

      c.   A march organization and formation is assembled.

2.   The March stage. (task)

      a.   Movement to and down the sidewalk of Hollywood Boulevard.

      b.   People on sidewalk move to the side, making room.

      c.   Traffic stopped at intersections.

      d.   Two moving motor cycles.

3.   The Termination stage. (divergence)

      a.   Members begin to desert march.

      b.   March back to park.

      c.   General breakdown of march three blocks from park — as unorganized stream movement emerges out of the march formation.

      d.   Remaining members return to park are ones with cars in area — most go immediately in groups of 1 to 5 to their cars.

      e.   The area is empty.

The empirical analysis of collective behavior situations via the observing and recording of changing spatial forms, provides the observer with a means for systematically finding/creating order in what, at first glance, appears as undifferentiated mass behavior. The above task career outline is a particularly helpful procedure to use in this enterprise. By comparison it shows that the usual terms used to describe various events, e.g., demonstrations, riot, confrontation, have very little empirical content or behavioral reference. They gloss over, rather than provide, understanding of unfolding interactions. More importantly, the distinctions and methods described, provide a basis for further empirical and theoretical work.

But before we can demonstrate the empirical and the theoretical advantages of this approach (Chapters 4 and 5 respectively), more foundational understanding must be established. Task forms are just one of two types of group form. The group form level of social organization emergent in collective assemblies also involves —crowd forms.

NOTES

1. Sam Wright, Field Notes, Rose Parade, Pasadena, California (January 1, 1974).

2. These people represent one type of a milling pattern which will be more fully described in the next chapter. Milling is a crowd form frequently found in connection with large collectivities.

3. Piling: to move or press forward in or as if in a mass crowd (Webster's *New Collegiate Dictionary,* 8th ed., Springfield, Mass.: G. C. Merriam and Co., 1973).

4. Neil Smelser, *Theory of Collective Behavior* (New York: The Free Press, 1963), p. 133.

5. Ralph H. Turner and Lewis M. Killian, *Collective Behavior,* 2nd ed. (Englewood Cliffs, N.J.: Prentice-Hall, 1972), p. 63.

6. Sam Wright, Field Notes, 1970.

7. From the first-had observations of Henry M. Knawls describing escalation of the Watts' Riot, in Jerry Cohen and William S. Murphy's *Burn, Baby, Burn* (New York: Avon Books, 1966), pp 99-105.

8. Viewing as a crowd activity rather than as a task activity is discussed in the next chapter.

9. Sam Wright, Field Notes, January 23, 1971.

CHAPTER 3

HOW CROWD FUNCTIONS
AFFECT GROUP FORM

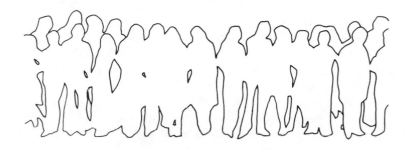

INTRODUCTION

After a few months of field work, I began to experience a sense deja vu. Unfolding social situations would 'be' familiar. They would have a "I've seen this before!" quality about them. Oddly enough, this sensing of the familiar took place independent of whatever was the reason (task) for the collective assembly. Pursuing the source of this 'order,' led my own attention away from the task performers. Instead, the behavior of those who were present in the situation, but not participating in collective task activities, came to occupy my thoughts and observations.

At any one point in time, the percentage of people in a situation who are engaged in task activities can vary widely. As a scene of collective behavior develops, people who had been moments before at the center of task activities, can find themselves suddenly out of the action. Further changes can return these people to participating in a collective task, or they can remain outside for the duration of the event. Others can arrive on the scene and spend their whole relationship engaged in activities other than task ones.

The object of this section is to consider these unobtrusive others. That is, people who are engaged in other than task activities. The activities of the nontask performers we shall call **crowd (adjunct) activities.** The configurations of their spatial distribution are crowd (adjunct) forms. Two of these should create a sense of deja vu in the reader. They are the convergence and the divergence forms. This section addresses the relationship between crowd function and crowd forms.

CROWD FORM AND FUNCTION

From event to event, there is a remarkable consistency in the type and number of collective activities that are engaged in by nontask performers. As a consequence, the spatial forms emergent from these crowd functions are few in number and readily identifiable. This is a reflection of the limited number of action alternatives available to nontask performers in the situation. That is, the activities that people can engage in that do not disrupt the on-going task activities. For if they were to become disruptive they would no longer be adjunct behaviors. They would become a new focus for collective task activities.

These adjunct performers can be involved in one of the following crowd functions:

1. Converging: moving into the scene, or

2. Viewing: watching others carry out task activities, or

3. Milling: Pursuing whatever individually obtainable ends are possible in this situation, e.g., talking, waiting, engaging in coquetry, trying to get into the task action, waiting for the task to begin, etc., or

4. Diverging: leaving the area altogether.

Because the nondisruptive options are limited, so are the activities to be engaged in, and consequently, so are the forms manifested by crowd members. Therefore, when one approaches an unfolding incident of collective behavior, there is always the sense of the familiar. For while types of task activities can vary immensely between situations, as noted in the last chapter, adjunct activities begin to repeat themselves.

THE BASIC CROWD FORMS

VIEWING FORMS

In the Rose Parade the *interdependent* relationship between audience and paraders was examined. This was seen to be such that, without one the other could not be. Therefore, audience activities were classified as a task activity essential to the task characteristics of the event. But, in the following, account #5 (Dead Man at the Beach), this is not the case.

In the "dead man incident," the viewers, a "circular form," encapsulated all the task performers. But the task performers could have carried out their tasks independently of the presence of the viewers. Though the task activities did have an *interactional* relation with the viewing activities, it was not one of interdependence.

The small and fixed space needs of the task activities (resuscitation, electric shock, injections) influenced the viewing form. The pragmatic problems which individuals encountered in viewing, which determined their orientation to one another, were in response to the spatial activity needs of the task performers. On the other hand, the viewers only influenced the task performers by negotiating and creating a limited work space for their activities.

DESCRIPTIVE ACCOUNT #5: DEAD MAN AT THE BEACH[1]

A block from the beach, a siren screaming — red Fire Department van, passed me by. When I got half way down the block, I could see a crowd gathering in the beach parking lot. Two police black and white units passed by, each sliding to a stop at the side of the crowd. I entered a beach-front store, bought a writing pad and a pen, and came out to take notes. Being a sociologist is definitely not a natural occupation. My swim and "time out" from social obligations would have to wait.

Except where the Emergency Paramedic Van blocked the view, the quitely excited and talking spectators formed a circle in the lot. I approached and joined the circle of nude backs, in a tight shoulder-to-shoulder formation. A quick count revealed that there were approximately 85 curiously craning spectators in a depth of from four to nine people. The open space in the middle of these viewers contained the two policemen, two paramedics, and the one lifeguard, all working on the one prone, and unmoving man in red swim trunks.

Converging individuals, and groups of two to four, came towards us with quickened steps from all directions. But these converging people were few in number compared to the population of sunbathers in sight. In fact, most people came from the ranks of those who were promenading on the boardwalk, which was approximately 15 feet away. However, only a small percentage of the promenaders came to join the crowd. Nevertheless, the number of spectators grew at a rate of about 10 to 12 people per minute, with a loss of about 3 people per minute.

While the medics frantically worked on the man, two "witnesses" moved outside the formation and began giving testamonial accounts of what had occurred and what was presently occurring. (I never learned the formal coroners account. According to the two "eye witnesses" 1. He drown while swimming 2. He died of a heart attack while jogging). Around the outside of the spectators, moving, peering, and talking groups emerged. They were made up of: (1) the old hands giving testimony; (2) new arrivals, who would either (a) seek information and then join the spectators, or (b) join the spectators and then seek information; (3) those leaving the spectators who would frequently mill about after separating themselves from the main formation; (4) those who would move from spot to spot at the rear of the formation — getting views from every angle; (5) a half dozen preteenagers on their bikes; and (6) some people who just seemed more at ease moving about behind.

Viewers are not instrumentally related to the carrying out of a task. This creates a distinction between the relations that they have with task performers and the relation that audiences have as interdependent task performers. This is due to the formal role that audiences are required to assume in relation to the task activities they have come to see.

Viewers, on the other hand, are engaged in crowd activities. The viewers are dependent upon the presence of task activities for providing them with something to view. *The task activities are not dependent upon these viewers. Viewers do not provide anything structurally essential to the carrying out of the task performance.* Because these two groups are present in the same spatial setting, there are mutual interaction effects, but not mutual dependencies.

During the homosexual-protest career, several nontask viewer relations appeared. At the police station, late arriving homosexuals took up viewing behaviors on the street corners, rather than joining in with the picketers. Marching down Hollywood Boulevard created "involuntary" viewers out of those exposed to the moving formation. Viewing forms can come into being through a variety of interactional processes. By examining some of the basic ones, dynamics can be added to our discussion.

PROCESSES OF CROWD VIEWER FORMATION

The common forms of collective viewing can emerge out of different processes. As a consequence, similar viewing forms can have different situated meanings by virtue of how they come into being. The first three of the five forms discussed are of special sociological interest.

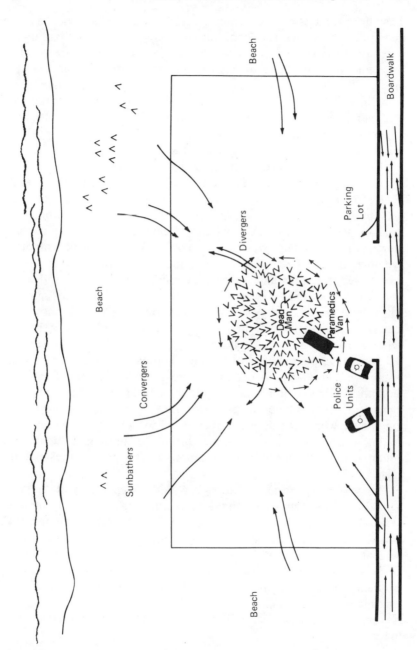

Figure 3.1   Dead man at the beach

They are products of interactions in which viewing behavior is more determined by structural conditions than by motivational factors.

1. Involuntary Viewers. One common reason marching protesters have adopted this form of activity is its effectiveness in creating viewers. People doing normal activities in public places find themselves to be involuntary viewers of moving protest marchers. Normal foot traffic and auto traffic is often disrupted, making the protest formation a pragmatic problem for the walkers and drivers. Their problem solving requires attention focusing on the protesters, i.e., they become involuntary viewers of the marching demonstrators.

There are many other interactional factors involved in the creation of this relationship. Noisy activity can force attention on itself by preventing other activities, e.g., conversation, concentration, etc., from taking place. By blocking a building entrance, sitting in, picketing, viewers are created by physical coercion. By displaying inflammatory symbols, marchers attract attention and make people viewers despite themselves, e.g., long hair on males, nonconforming dress, and so on.

2. The Residual Viewer. This viewer form frequently appears when there are too many people present to fill the limited number of task positions available at the present developmental stage of the task activity. The storming of a building, or the looting of one as in Account #2, can place the majority of the people present in viewer relations. There is not enough physical space proximate to the area of entry for more than a limited number of people. For the same reason, the actual hanging phase of a lynching produces viewing behavior on the part of the people who were previously engaged in the task activities, e.g., getting a rope, storming a jail, etc. In the "dead man incident," the volunteers to help the victim far outnumbered the possibilities of doing such.

The viewer relations resulting are still independent of the task behavior. The viewers do have a facilitating effect on the task performers. The presence of others willing to fill a vacated task position, increases the value of the position. This also encourages dedication on the part of the task performers by increasing their status as position occupants. Furthermore, the presence of viewers, as frequently noted in the literature,[2] is supportive of an interpretation of legitimacy, acceptance, and approval of the task being carried out. Nevertheless, the task can still be successfully implemented without these viewers.

3. Locationally Convenient Viewing Areas. Certain locations in relation to a performing collectivity continually develop into viewing areas. Office building windows, roof tops, balconies, and any of a variety of elevated places are used by people for viewing. These areas create audiences by offering convenient locations for viewing to those who would otherwise not take the time or effort to do so.

4. Intermittent Viewers. Viewers are often created, and always reinforced and maintained by those who are using the viewing relations for more than just viewing. In the Century Plaza Hotel account to follow, it was observed how task performers would drop into viewing roles in order to rest. When the homosexuals reached the police sation, a sizable proportion of the leadership formed into viewing relations and guided the task activities from there. Also, the police, throughout the homosexual-Nazi confrontation remained passively in viewer relation. Activities that can be carried out under the guise of viewing are only limited by imagination.

5. The Snowball Effect. Once begun, viewing relations can be maintained and grow through processes independent of any actual task activities taking place. That is to say, the viewing form becomes a social object in and of itself, which gains attention and draws interpretations from outside. Passersby, frequently, cannot see "what is going on." But, if they cannot see what is going on, they are assuming something is going on. This assumption stems from the reading of the presence of viewing form. This is taken as a sign that something is occurring. Milgram[3] has done a study relating the interactional snowball effect of the size of a viewing form to its attractive value. His findings indicate that size is interpreted as a sign of the degree of significance of that which the viewers are assumed to be looking. Large groups grow at a faster rate than smaller ones. Once a form reaches a certain size, then the self-fulfilling prophecy is at work — i.e., a crowd grows rapidly larger as people interpret its already large size as being a sign of something of particular significance. This increase in its size, making it even larger than before, causes more people to be attracted, etc. This interaction effect is nonmonotonic and U-shaped with growth not keeping up with losses after a certain saturation point is reached.

THE MILLING FORM

Around the outside of the viewer form, in the "dead man incident," individuals stood and/or moved about, not focusing on the task activity. The basic body orientation for the movers were: (1) shoulders to the backs of the viewers, (2) moving or eddying about and around the viewers' circular periphery, (3) stopping and orienting the body so that (a) they could view the task activities, (b) they became stationary millers (involved in talking), and (c) they would be facing outward. For the stationary millers, their orientations were: (1) towards one another in conversational semicircular clusters of two to four; (2) stationary; (3) at different angles of orientation to the viewers according to locations in clusters. The overall configuration was of a shifting or milling ring around the viewers — that was approximately eight to ten feet wide. Individual distances were greater among the millers than the viewers. Thus, the milling form had the appearance of permeability until one came to the solid outside boundary of the viewer form.

In the parade account (#1), milling relations occurred between the grandstand and the curbside audience. The movers dominated this representation of milling such that two streams of moving millers emerged with only occasional clusters of standing types. During the welfare rally (account # 6), we find the millers to be located between the viewers and performers. This group was dominated by all moving members.

DESCRIPTIVE ACCOUNT #6: WELFARE RALLY[4]

The top of the steps, leading from the mall into the County Administration Building, was the site of the speakers' microphone. Chairs were set in a rectangle of rows of 10 by 15. These faced the microphone with the first row of chairs being approximately 20 feet from the speakers' podium. When the chairs were filled, people lackadaisically began sitting on the low cement ledges to the sides of the chairs, running perpendicular to the speakers' podium.

Groups of teenagers began to restlessly move about between the audience and speakers. These were unusually large moving groups of between 6 and 12. They moved in tight, intimately close clusters. Later, I found out that at least two of these groups were gangs "waiting for some action." There were approximately 20 people on the dias, 200 spectators, and 35 moving Black and Chicano gang members. It drizzled all afternoon. The rally fizzled. Everyone was bored including the speakers.

In sum: the milling form is that configuration of people who are
(1) not interdependently related to the task activity; (2) not focusing
their activities on the task activities, i.e., they are not viewing; (3) but
are engaged in moving or standing activities in relation to the task

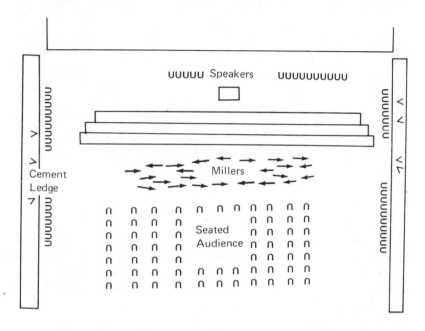

Figure 3.2 Welfare rally

activities such that they do have an emergent form, and the task,
viewer, and milling forms interactionally influence one another.
Because of the freedom from the need to view task activities, milling
will appear in a variety of spatial relations relative to the task activity
forms.

The crowd milling relations so far discussed can be analytically
distinguished from crowd milling phases of task activities, although
both are crowd and not task activities. Crowd milling phases of task
activities are differentiated from the basic crowd milling form in that
they are bracketed, temporarily, and are experienced as such. They
appear as, and have meaning in terms of their location, as phases of
development in an unfolding event. The detailed form analysis of the

homosexual protest reveals that milling occurrred before the event and at its final termination period. It also occurred during the transition period when returnees from the protest were milling in the park, waiting for the next task activity to emerge.

Beside the milling among task performers, in the phases of initiation, transition, and termination, audiences also go through phases of milling behavior. McPhail has indicated that audiences regularly go through phases of noncollective focusing.[5] This is normally in response to breaks in the presenting career of task performances, e.g., between speakers, between acts, between events. This milling is also distinguishable from the basic crowd milling as being a phase in the task event. The basic crowd milling goes on continuously and independently of the task-hiatus-crowd milling. It is a form that has an entity status of its own in a task situation.

PROCESS OF MILLING FORMATION

As with the viewing audience and task forms, close inspection reveals that milling as a crowd form comes into being through several different processes. All reflect the dominant characteristic of crowd milling behavior. They show people to be in pursuit of individually attainable ends.

1. **Milling for Meaning.** At emergent events, information seeking and/or definition of the situation construction, is a major activity. While people will join an audience or viewers to make inquiries or to see for themselves, milling forms will often emerge to serve this function. During the "dead man incident," testifiers appeared who greeted newcomers and provided an oral history of the event to date. These historians were accompanied by emergent intellectuals who provided reasoned accounts on the medical/life-saving activities.

2. **Milling and Body Needs Satisfaction.** Planned and emergent events which last more than half an hour naturally produce milling behavior as people begin to attend to natural body needs. The obvious body needs are for food, water, and elimination. Here the relation of milling to need satisfaction is that of a means to an end. But, equally important, are the body needs that are satisfied in the act of milling itself.

The need to stretch, to take a break from viewing, or task performing, or to burn off nervous energy, can swell the ranks of the millers. Age becomes an important variable in this. Matinee time at the local neighborhood theater is remarkable for the number of kids that can be running in the aisles at any one moment. There are times when they appear to outnumber the audience in the seats.

Sexual/courtship needs get their older brothers and sisters milling (see account #1). Boredom can set mothers and fathers to milling about. The need to stretch can get grandparents on the move.

3. **Milling Form as A Mixture of Different Activities.** In the welfare situation (#6), the avowed intent of the millers was the "looking for action." In other events, there is a mixture of reasons for engaging in this behavior. At one riot, I observed the following types of people to be simultaneously present among the millers, between the viewing form and those involved in the task of attacking the building. There were those seeking an opening to join into the fray as well as counter-rioters who were hauling away the ripped-off doors of the building, so that they could not be used as missiles or clubs. There were two undercover police whom I had seen at many such events. There were also a number of people so caught in the excitement that attempts to engage them in interaction revealed that they were literally not capable of conscious interpretive reflection. At that point in time a good proportion of the protest leadership was among the millers — apparently to avoid arrest. There were a number of individuals who seemed to have a push-pull fascination with the task performers — such that they would compulsively move to the front of the millers and then back off to the audience and then back in again, in a never ending yo-yo pattern of movement, and one high school girl taking notes like myself, for a paper she had to write.

CONVERGENCE — DIVERGENCE

As discussed in Chapter 2, converging and diverging forms are most informative. A "stranger" encountering one or the other understands that collective task activity is going to occur or has occurred. At the site of a scheduled event, the emergence of convergence forms is a sign that the event will soon start, of the approximate size that it will be, etc. And, as found in the next account, an increase in the number of people diverging from an event, often signals its de facto termination.

DESCRIPTIVE ACCOUNT #7: PRESIDENT NIXON PROTEST[6]

I am a little behind schedule. Already there is more than a normal amount of foot traffic heading towards the hotel. Ha! A huge military helicopter is landing. The President is missing his chance to greet the welcoming crowd by arriving early.

There are now steady streams of people coming from every direction joining into the massive, chanting, circling demonstration. The mood is up, people are excited yet serious. Past police confrontations here have been too bloody to allow too much to be taken for granted.

Other than the 30 policemen visible in the lights of the hotel entrance, this massive crowd is, literally, demonstrating to tiers of empty balconies that lined and columned the face of the building (a sure sign that those inside were aware of our presence). It had been at least half an hour since the last guest had arrived.

There were now 300 to 350 people standing and milling in my area across the street from the hotel.

Between us and the hotel, there are between three and four thousand people. They have been moving in a clockwide direction. They formed one gigantic circle of picketing and chanting protesters. The circle of bodies moved down the sidewalk on this side of the street and back on the other side. The circlers were two to six abreast, with very little distance between the ranks. From my elevated position, I see light streams of people, steadily entering and leaving the area. Also, off in the side streets to this area, clusters of standing and talking people were dimly visible. Many people use the area, where I am, as a place for an intermission or a rest stop, from the demonstrating.

People are beginning to tire. Chants are less frequent and vocal. Exodus is taking place in every direction as people are now slowly streaming away from the hotel.

In-migration or convergence has basic individual orientations of (1) shoulder to shoulder, (2) facing toward the focus, while (3) moving and being oriented, in (4) a face-to-back relationship with those ahead, and (5) a back-to-face relationship with those behind.

Out-migration or divergence involves the same individual orientation as the *in*-migration or convergence, with the difference being that the outwardly migrating people are facing away from the task activity area.

A consequence of the spatial converging brought about by *in*-migration is that the distance between individuals and their basic orientations in relations to one another decreases. The net effect is an increase in density, usually accompanied by a slowing of movement and in extreme situations, a massing of bodies into a compact piling form. *Out*-migration reverses the processes with the opposite consequences.

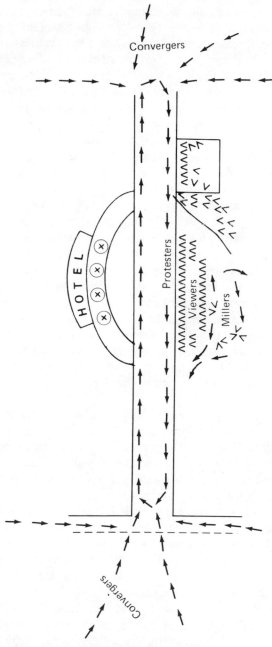

Figure 3.3 President Nixon protest

Migration from one point to another is one of the most common task activities engaged in collective behavior, e.g., a marching demonstration, a parade. Because of this, special care is required to distinguish nontask migration from task migration. In clearly defined events, such as The Nixon protest, the Rose parade, the welfare rally, and phases of the homosexual protest, movement into an area (before the event begins) and out of the area (after the event is terminated) are clearly phases of converging and diverging nontask activities.

During the homosexual protest the movement of people between the park and the police station were also nontask converging and diverging activities. At the termination of the rally, the announcement was made to reassemble at the police station. Through divergence and convergence took on a collective form, they were crowd forms. Throughout the "Dead Man at the Beach" incident adjunctive converging and diverging continually took place. The same patterns appeared at the Nixon protest.

Task migrations are those movements of people in which the movement from a place (A) to some other place (B), becomes an activity to be accomplished collectively. The parade performers in the Rose Parade were task migrators. The march activity of the homosexual protest was a task activity. Prior to a Chicano riot, reported on in the next chapter, there was a rally. It was followed by an organized march to the L.A.P.D. headquarters. This stands in contrast as a task activity to the crowd movement of the homosexuals from a rally to a police station.

Converging and diverging always stand in the relational career phases as the bracketing forms around a task form i.e., convergence, task, divergence. These two forms are also frequently present in lesser density throughout an event, as late arrivals and early departures straggle in and out of the area. In the next section we shall again turn to process to describe crowd form development.

Processes of Convergence and Divergence. The process by which people come to converge and diverge from planned events are routinized. Information is usually obtained during some time period before an event through formal and informal channels of communication. People converge accordingly. When the event officially terminates, people normally respond by leaving the area.

But other processes can also become involved. This is true of both planned and unplanned events, and especially for convergence. Three of these interactional factors are briefly presented below.

1. *Location and Traditional Migratory Patterns.* Planners of events will use normal foot traffic paths of movement as a resource for "attracting" people not already involved in their event. At Berkeley, during the Free Speech Movement, rallies were held near the main paths in and out of the campus at the times of their highest rates of use. These periods of heavy traffic brought people into the rallies who were bent on totally different ends.

In the "dead man incident," it was described how the passersby made up the greatest proportion of those who converged on the task scene. Sunbathers, who were equally as close but engaged in different activities, were not attracted at anywhere near the same rate.

As noted under the viewer form section, the more direct blocking of traffic paths forces the people into this role. This accomplishment is a consequence of the placing of an event such that the converging people are immigrating to an event without their knowledge.

2. *Territorial Range.* Public places seldom exist without being acclaimed preserves of various groups and individuals. An occurrence within a public place consequently becomes an occurrence within someone's bailiwick. Those who wander these areas, as their normal activity — gangs, old people, street corner societies, store owners on their blocks — become nontask **in-**or **out**-migrators reacting to territorial invasions and not convergers to the task activities for participation reasons.

3. *The Pragmatic Migrators.* As always, the various reasons for movement toward any event must take into account those who see it as a chance to pursue their own ends, independent of the event. These can range from pickpockets to people looking for pick-ups. This categorization of immigration has no limits other than the enterprising individuals and their ingenuity. Crowds are seen as the place "where the action is."

THE CAREER OF A VIEWING FORM

With the fundamental description of crowd forms completed, attention can be directed to the history of crowd forms. As with task forms, crowd forms also have developmental careers. Any crowd activity goes through various phases in response to changes in task activities and in response to problems encountered in carrying out the crowd activity itself.

In the account which follows, a detailed look over time is provided for one set of viewing relations. Herein are found four typical factors in viewing behavior: (1) viewing is usually associated with an area which is higher than the scene of task activities; (2) viewing areas have to be negotiated and this can involve several stages; (3) viewing activities and their manifested forms are passed on to newcomers as "old-timers" leave; and (4) viewers can become engaged in task activities, thereby losing their viewer status and consequently being treated as actives.

DESCRIPTION #8: DEMONSTRATION: CENTURY PLAZA HOTEL[7]

I arrived an hour early to walk, map, an survey the area. I began to look for a headquarters to work out of. Experience had taught me that large-scale events required a vantage point for observation. Without this, major interactional sequences can come or go without my knowledge. I found the perfect location across the four-laned street from the hotel.

There was a sloping incline, covered with small plants, going from the sidewalk up to a walkway in front of the building which opposed the hotel. The elevation of the incline was approximately 15 feet. The walkway, in front of the building, was approximately 10 feet wide by 25 paces long. More importantly, from the walkway there was access to a 15 by 65 foot roof of a structure that occupied a corner of this property. Though a cul de sac, it offered a great overview of the hotel across the street and the full length of the block in both directions.

As the protesters began to arrive and to start their circling below, the negotiating process for the viewing area began. The first people to come up the incline were from the as of yet, thin line of the protesters. They commented on how the protest activities had not yet really started. Then they adopted viewing relations to the scene below. After half an hour, the number of those people swelled to about 80 and overflowed from the walkway onto the plant covered incline. At this time, building guards, who had been watching, received orders to clear us away. This was accomplished with little grumbling. These people moved down and joined the circling protesters.

Less than four minutes later, new people spied this natural area and began to drift up from below. Within 15 minutes, the walkway was again filled, the plants inundated, and seven male teenagers had crossed over onto the roof structure that was level with the walkway. The building police then received orders to clear the area of this crowd of onlookers. They met some resistance and protesters below yelled up supportive words to us who were being evicted.

Within minutes, a third wave of totally new people began to drift into this area. By this time, the number of protesters had reached about 2,000. It was growing rapidly. The increased rate of inflow up the incline and the filling of the area, reflected this. While the second wave, was four-fifths couples and one-fifth teenagers, the third wave was approximately one-half couples, and one-quarter teenagers of both sexes, and one-quarter young men in their twenties, ranging in appearance from a few hippies to the well, but casually dressed middle-class types.

The building police made one last effort to exert some control. They attempted to, and succeeded in clearing the roof of the structure of approximately 25 males. But no sooner had they left the roof unguarded than the invasion began again in earnest. This time a few females joined the males on the roof of the structure, the incline was totally covered with people and the walkway packed such that it was difficult to move. The building police were seen no more.

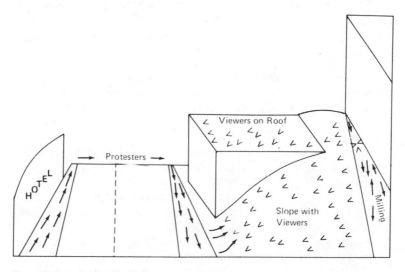

Figure 3.4 Established viewer form

The presence of several viewing formations located around task forms is a common pattern. Three separate viewing groups coalesced on the same side of the picketers as the one being described. On the hotel side of the picketers there were two more groups of viewers. A significant difference existed between the groups on each side.

The three viewer formations across from the hotel were basically alike in terms of types of participants, means of joining membership, and the use made of them. On the hotel side the two viewing groups were as different from one another as they were from the three across the way. One group was of police officers only. They were in full riot gear and viewed as a means of passing the time until they might be called to task action.

The other viewer formation contained at various times, newspaper and television reporters and cameramen, hotel guests, arriving dinner guests, secret service men, hotel officials, etc. The casual viewer was blocked from entry into either formation. A few police were posted to restrict access to both viewer formation.

In many types of collective assembly, viewers forms are differentiated along some situational set of values e.g., beliefs, demographic characteristics. In potential situations of confrontation, these differences are even more likely to be present. And as the following indicates, these differences can have consequences for the interactions between groups:

> While all this was occurring, guests were constantly arriving in large black limousines. The circling protesters were chanting and yelling at each of the cars as they made their turn towards the hotel entrance. At the height of this, the number of moving people reached approximately 4,000.
>
> About 20 minutes after the last move by the building police, I observed among those on the incline, three extremely well-dressed males in their late twenties, drinking beer. When they brought two cartons of eggs out of a bag, I began to make escape plans. As the next limousine made the turn toward the hotel, a volley of white eggs arched their way through the air. A collective "Ooh" of appreciation and foreboding came from the circle of protesters, who had, themselves, been yelling and chanting at this latest arrival.
>
> There was no time to lament the fact that every egg missed its mark. A phalanx of 17 officers had immediately begun to cross from the hotel entrance toward us. The protesters between hurriedly parted from the path of the running officers. Most of the protesters stopped their moving, turned and faced us. From them, a massive outcry of yelling and shouting began and was directed at the police as they started up the incline.

The normal pandemonium that accompanies a charge by the police was taking place among those who, a few minutes before, had been spectators. Women were screaming in fright, as, in a mad rush of movement, everyone tried to disassociate themselves from the area. The police ran up the incline, trapping those who had not gotten away, against the wall of the building. Only a few were beaten before a recall order was given and the police went back to the hotel.

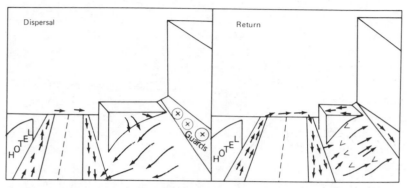

Figure 3.5 Patters of dispersal by building guards and viewer return

Darkness was falling. A late arriving limousine reoriented the protesters' attention back to the street and their original task activities. Except for a dozen high school kids, the audience area immediately emptied when the police arrived; but, within five minutes, the area began to fill again. Three distinct sections developed within the area, during this final invasion stage. The roof slowly filled with teenagers and long hairs; the trampled incline became filled with couples dropping out of the circling protesters. The walkway became an area of much movement and conversation and very little audience behavior.

These actions were a fascinating example of group "role reversal." The picketers who before had been the task group became viewers. The two previously viewing groups became the participants in the new collective task interaction. Upon the successful dispersal of the losing group of the confrontation, all groups returned to their original activities.

For the next two hours, the turnover of population in all three sections of the viewing area, appeared to take place in approximately twenty-minute periods. The incline and walkway were particularly effective in

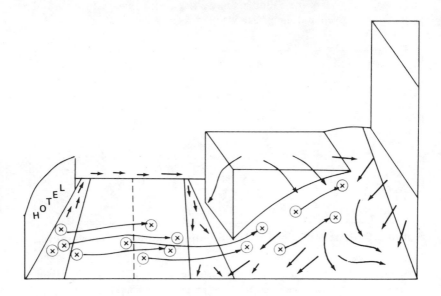

Figure 3.6   Invasion by L.A.P.D. after egg throwing

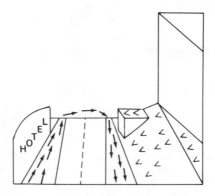

Figure 3.7   Final reestablishment of viewing form

passing on the viewing and milling relations to newcomers as the old-timers moved on. The roof had a group of about 15 grass smokers who were less inclined toward movement. In the middle of the second hour, the number of new members was not keeping up with the number of those moving on. At the end of the third hour, the audience had dwindled down to 12 of us on the roof. Below, clusters of conversing people were randomly distributed in the sidewalks. The protest was over.

This particular set of viewing activities and so its viewing form, had a full and rich career. It was dispersed twice by building guards before the third reformation established the viewer sovereignty over the area. Even then, the guards made one last effort to control the viewers by clearing the roof. The egg-throwing incident turned viewers into task stars. The resulting third clearing of the area, this time by the city police, made it possible for the fourth and final viewer form to be established.

Other sequences of behavior simultaneously developed. The size, shape, and density of the viewing form went through several stages. Despite its many interruptions, the form tended to follow a normal curve in growth. It was largest in number and size and most dense during the middle time period of the protest. All three of these variables were of smaller magnitude at the beginning and end of the protest.

The complete turnover of the viewers in approximately 20-minute periods continued consistently throughout the evening. That is, after the last dispersal took place, the natural flow was allowed to follow its course. Whether or not the earlier phase of the activity would have followed this pattern is a matter of speculation. Finally, there is enough evidence to indicate that major demographic composition shifts occurred over time, e.g., the decrease in the number of couples and the increase in the number of teenagers. But, my observational notes did not consistently report on this. It will have to suffice for the present to point out the existence of this phenomena.

The career of this one viewing form is the history of a group. The interactions that have been described are of two types. One set of interactions centered around the processes of this groups' formation. The other interactions were of this group in various relationships with other groups in the situation.

The group, inter-group relationship, and group characteristics underlie most of the materials presented up till this point. In order to conceptually integrate Chapter 2 and 3, our discussion will now directly address the role of the group in collective assemblies. There could be no more fitting manner to do this, than to begin with some thoughts of Emile Durkheim.

TASK AND CROWD FORMS: A SYSTEM OF GROUP RELATIONS

Emile Durkheim, in *The Rules of the Sociological Method,* provides standards for identifying and analyzing "social facts." The prime principle is that, we are to study social facts as a level of phenomena that is not reducible to the individuals that comprise it.[8]

> Whenever certain elements combine and thereby produce, by the fact of their combination, new phenomena, it is plain that these new phenomena reside not in the original elements but in the totality formed by their union.[9]

The basic qualities that these social facts must have, are,

1) tendencies to "permanencies" over time,[10]

2) operations independent of their content,[11]

3) the characteristics of "things" with features independent of our own mental thoughts or ideas about them,[12]

4) qualities "external to individuals,"[13] and

5) "constraining" upon individual behaviors and thougths.[14]

Individuals are constrained to conform to the emergent reality:

> Since this joint activity takes place outside each one of us (for a plurality of consciousnesses enter into it), its necessary effect is to fix, to institute outside of us, certain ways of acting and certain judgements which do not depend on each particular will taken separately.[15]

Do group forms meet these criteria? First, group forms exist solely at the level of social facts. These spatial configurations emerge out of collectivities of individuals standing in social and spatial relationship to one another. These configurations are not reducible to any individual behavior or characteristics. Group forms are recurrent, permanent features of all incidences of collective assembly. They have empirically determinable and verifiable characteristics similar to material "things," e.g., shape, size, movements, developmental processes, and so on.

Finally group forms exist externally to and are constraining on the members who produce them. This is such that people in one formation are *normatively* expected to conform to behaviors that are different from behaviors in another form. Audience members should not begin parading and vice versa. Viewers should not engage in rock throwing task activities or they will lose their collective exemption status from police "sanctioning" reprisals.

Having established the nature of your social facts, Durkheim states that a classification into social types is then in order.[16] This classification must be constructed from "essential characteristics" derived from the social fact level and not individual characteristics. A typology of group forms has been constructed by taking spatial relationships and body orientations between individuals as the minimum unit of analysis. Convergence, milling, viewing, and divergence are resultant crowd types. Each kind of task activity produces its own form and these in turn can be typologized as parades, looting, or rallies.

With the completion of these steps, we are now in the position to describe the social/spatial system of collective assemblies. We will see that groups and their forms are the constituent, functioning elements of these systems of social relationships. This objective can best be gained by reexamining two assumptions of prior collective behavior theories.

It is argued here, that previous crowd theorists have erred in two basic ways. These are in terms of their *scope of focus* and their reliance on one *level of analysis*. Let us begin with the problem of scope.

Most prior theorists have limited their empirical and theoretical focus to just the active task participants on one side of an event, e.g., rioters. In effect, these task performers have been analyzed as if they were operating in an interactional vacuum. In order to minimumly understand the interactional relations between the task activities of agents of social control, e.g., the police, and the rioters, one would have to include both within a common focus of analysis. If this scope were used, then outcomes of a "riot" would be explained in terms of the processes and careers of the interactions between the two task groups.

For the most part, instead of this, the behavior of rioters has been examined for situated cause. Thus, we are offered explanatory schemes that deal solely with emotional contagion or imitation among the rioters or the convergence of predisposed to riot people to an area, or the emergent norms among the rioters. It is suggested that the total system of relations in the situation, and the complexities of their interaction, is a more relevant scope of focus.

The second major difficulty with prior perspectives also, in part, underlies the first problem. Collective behavior theorists have predominately dealt with only individual behavior and characteristics and not the sociological group level of reality. As a consequence two of the three explanatory theoretical perspectives of collective behavior have failed to deal with the most basic fact of collective behavior — that collective behavior is group behavior and for the most part, it can be analyzed in terms of groups interacting with other groups.[17]

With these two factors in mind, let us return to Durkheim's discussion of the group. After typologizing, he states that we must look at "The nature and number of the component elements and their mode of combination."[18] It is these elements in interaction that make up a system of relations. And it is this system that we have been building through Chapter 2 and 3.

In these chapters, we have, (1) delineated the types of structural groups to be found in collective behavior, (2) demonstrated how these groups emerge out of individual behavior, (3) shown how each group has a career of existence over time, (4) detailed how groups stand in interactional and interdependent relationships to other groups, and (5) depicted some of the patterns of emergence and diffusion of groups over the history of a collective behavior event.

This was accomplished by working at the emergent level of "social facts." Thus the importance of group form in actual interaction and for analysis becomes clear. Form is an "essential characteristic" of the emergent level. Members of collective assemblies and objective observers use group forms to identify groups and group functions. (And, as we shall see in the next chapter, form also has an independent effect on collective actions.)

In the process of making the above points, important facts about the structure of the systems of group relationships have been gained. During the task dominated phases of collective assemblies, there is normally a distinctive *group division of labor*. Task groups, viewing groups, milling, converging and diverging groups are present in various numbers and combinations. These groups, standing in relation to one another, make up the system which should be included in any comprehensive scope of analysis.

These groups continually influence one another in various degrees. When task accomplishment requires more than one group, as in the parade, there is a high degree of mutual influence. The interdependence of the activities assures this. Viewing and milling groups are dependent on task groups and so directly effected. They in turn have interactional effects on task activities, but not structurally determinable ones. Interaction between all combinations of groupings within a setting is the emergent sociological level of analysis.

The fluidness of a groups' existence reflects the emergent dynamics of collective assemblies over time. By combining the findings on task and adjunct (crowd) groups, the structure of their relations in changing sequences of presentation is determinable. An inspection of the career form outline of the homosexual protest reveals a pattern: (1) converging behavior, (2) milling among the arrived convergers, followed by (3) emergent viewing and milling forms which became spatially oriented to, (4) the task activity which, upon its termination, gives rise to (5) divergent activity. This is a sequence repeated throughout the day. Converging, milling, viewing, task, and diverging is a standard career pattern of the interrelationship over time of crowd and task groups.

This is not to say that while a task form has emerged, converging forms are not in evidence. Nor, that any of the other forms cannot be present in the various phases dominated by another activity. On the contrary, that fact has been the focus of a large part of the discussion. However, the above sequences of development of these activities is basic to the phases.

In the account of the Century Plaza Hotel demonstration, people are first observed to be arriving in the area (converging). They proceed to stand, talking or move about on the sidewalk (milling). After a while, some people made their way up to the elevated area across the street from the hotel. From this vantage point, they look out over the convergers and millers below (viewing). Half an hour after the convergers began to appear a circling picket line is started in front of the hotel. Soon this has spread into a giant moving circle of protesters that extends the full length of the block on both sides of the street (task). Approximately an hour and a half after this, a noticeable number of people, individually or in twos or threes, begin to leave the area. For the next hour, there is a steady flow of exiting people which ultimately empties the space in front of the hotel (diverging). The reader is invited to inspect the other accounts throughout this book, or to observe the next collective assembly they attend, for evidence of this pattern.

Figure 3.8   (1) Converging (2) Milling (3) and (4) Viewing, milling and
task (5) Divergence

THE GROUP IN COLLECTIVE BEHAVIOR:
INTENTION AND ATTENTION TO FORM

Many occasions of collective assembly lack institutional or formal
organizational structure. As a consequence, most groups that emerge
under these circumstances also lack formal organization. There are
often no previously determined procedures or criteria for selection and
identification of members, for establishing channels of communication, selecting leadership, determining status hierarchies, or setting
goals. A mistake to be avoided in interpreting this is to take the absence
of formal structures of groups to be a sign of the absence of groups
themselves.

In addressing this issue, Turner and Killian caution against seeing
collectivities of actors as being nothing more than aggregations of
individuals:

> As a group, a collectivity is more than simply a number of individuals.
> A group always consists of people who are in interaction and whose
> interaction is affected by some sense that they constitute a unit.[19]

The basis, from which is derived the sense of being a unit or group can
vary. Turner and Killian, with their emphasis on verbal constructions
of reality, tend to stress shared opinions, beliefs, and definitions of the
situation. These are said to provide the conditions for the emergence of
group norms.

The argument developed here points to another means by which
people come to recognize and establish a sense of group — nonverbally.
From this perspective, behavior itself becomes that which is the
measure of group existence. Either individuals are behaviorally
oriented and acting in recognition of being part of a group or they are
not acting in this manner. This is another reason why group form takes
on such significance. Individual behavioral orientations readily tell if

persons are acting in terms of a sense of group. That is, have they assumed a behavioral orientation that conforms to this product of the group? My research, as reported here, indicates that indeed they do assume such relationships.

When people enter into a collective behavior situation, they routinely orient themselves to be spatially consistent with or in conformity to some collectivity of other bodies. They join the viewers or the millers or perhaps even a task group. If for some reason they do not wish to remain in the area, they might join a stream of divergers. This process involves the recognition of and the attending to the maintenance of the groups' form.

From this a conclusion is drawn. Most collectivities require members to give some attention to the group form that they embody and produce. This is the minimal membership dues for being in the collectivity. Even emergent activities such as looting or rock throwing provides anonymity and mutual support only so long as one sustains a proper spatial orientation to the collective form. This degree of attention demanded of collective assembly participants is of two types. The more general and inclusive type is simply the keeping of one's self within the shifting configuration or boundaries of the group. Many situations ask for no more from the participants. But some collective activities also require attention to the maintenance of a specific shape of the group form.

Waiting in line (queueing) behavior or parading, to be successful activities, require members to consciously maintain a linear form as a part of the process of carrying out the task. That is, these forms take members' conscious construction as a part of the implementation of the task activities. Lynching does not need this same detailed attention to the shape of the members' spatial arrangement.

Giving attention to an emergent form and form as a product of intention are distinct acts. Groups which require specific form maintenance have specific membership norms. Members are at a minimum accountable for sustaining consistency with the overall pattern and contributing to its production. Potential and actual group identity can be influenced by these factors. The categories below are presented as a tenative typology of the relational basis for the distinction between unintended and intended forms.

INTENTION AND FORM

I. Unintended
These are the spatial forms of collectivities which appear more or less without predesign. The relational basis for form emergence are:

1. Forms manifested from interactions with the practical-physical problems of a task accomplishment, e.g., moving from "X" to "B" in the looting incidents, convergence, divergence.

2. Subgroup forms emerging from interaction with other subgroup forms.

   a. Interdependent interaction, e.g., police-demonstrator confrontations rapidly develop into such unplanned activities as police giving chase to the demonstrators. The resulting group forms are basically unintended.

   b. One-way dependency, e.g., the viewer form at the police station was dependent upon the homosexual picketing form, but while the picketing form was planned, the viewing form emerged without the viewers' conscious design.

3. The overall form manifested from the interaction of all subgroup forms with one another. While subgroups may plan their forms within a collective assembly, the total, or overall patterns which are manifested during their interactions are frequently not considered, e.g., several groups moving from one place to another.

II. Intentional

There are forms that are conscious constructions of the actors. They can be found under any of the above relational circumstances. The ends to which people oriented themselves, so that a particular form emerges, are:

1. *Symbolic:* Marching with military precisions and formation in a parade is not done to make getting from point "A" to point "B" more efficient. It is a symbolic form display. Efficiency is a byproduct of the symbolic display of uniformity, collective purposefulness, and control.

2. *Perceived as legally mandated:* Laws can specify what forms can be used in public places. For the homosexual protest in the park, a permit was required which specifically stated what collective forms could be used, i.e., a speaker-audience interdependent one. The movement from the park to the police station had to meet city ordinances which limit the spatial form of the demonstrators, e.g., people had to be moving, on the sidewalk, leaving room for opposing foot traffic. At the station, itself, the protest was highly regulated. The only form that was legally permitted was a moving circle of picketing demonstrators.

3. *Created displays of a social order.* Some spatial forms are created for their use value as a form in and of itself. People orient themselves into queues, or a linear formation, so that:

a. an internal order of turn location is established, i.e., where you are in the linear form (a line) in relation to some payoff, such as a ticket window. This is contingent upon individuals being simultaneously oriented to the form created from their spatial orientation and in relationship to others' body orientations.

b. an externally visible form display is presented to be readable to outsiders. It is consciously produced by individuals out of their orientations to one another, as an intentional display of a collective spatial claim to the payoff. It is also presented as a form which can be read by outsiders as having an externally determinable end to which one can join one's own body orientation and become part of the intended order of the formation, e.g., any line from kindergartners at a water fountain to horse betters at the paramutual window or the audience (Rose Parade) formation has a similarly intended construction relative to good viewings positions.

4. *Perceived efficiency:* the rationalization of a collective task comes, in part, from attending to the spatial distribution of members that might otherwise occur without attention to form. By having people march in step, on line and in column, a more efficient moving of a collectivity from one place to another can be accomplished. Soldiers marching in formation during a parade are putting on public display what they routinely do as an expedient mode of collective movement.

5. *Pragmatically determined:* Some tasks can only successfully be managed when the collective form is consciously dealt with. The forming of a wagon train into a circle was a necessary form if a successful defense against attack was to be made.

6. *Direct social control:* Control of a collectivity of people by outsiders is obtained by controlling:

a. the spatial form they are required to be located and maintained in, and

b. their orientation to one another within this form, e.g., after the Attica Prison riot was ended, at one point, prisoners were stripped nude, herded into a large circular, massing of bodies and ordered to lie in a face-down prone head-to-toe orientation to other prisoners on the ground.[20]

So far analysis has concentrated on describing the "elements" of a system and their "modes of combination." But if indeed group interaction dominates collective assemblies, and if group forms characterize an essential feature of these groups, then it remains to be demonstrated how groups and their forms are actually engaged in a system of relevant moment-to-moment symbolic interactions. In the next chapter, accounts and explanations shift to the dynamics of the processes of interaction between groups via their group forms.

NOTES

1. Field Notes, Sam Wright, July 20, 1974, Venice Beach, Venice, California.
2. Orrine E. Klapp, *Currents of Unrest* (New York: Holt, Rinehart and Winston, Inc., 1972), p. 26.
3. S. Milgram and H. Toch, "Collective Behavior in Crowds and Social Movements," in *Handbook of Social Psychology,* Vol. 4, eds. G. Lindzey and E. Aaronson (Reading, Mass.: Addison Wesley, 1969), pp. 531-532.
4. Field Notes, Sam Wright, 1973.
5. Clark McPhail, *Some Theoretical and Methodological Strategies for the Study of Crowd Phenomena,* (Unpublished Manuscript), p. 7.
6. Sam Wright, Field Notes, May, 1972.
7. Sam Wright, Field Notes, May, 1972.
8. Emile Durkheim, *The Rules of Sociological Method,* (The Free Press, New York, 1964), p. 13.
9. Ibid., p. xlvii.
10. Ibid., p. xviii.
11. Ibid., p. l.
12. Ibid., p. xliii.
13. Ibid., p. xlvii.
14. Ibid., p. liii.
15. Ibid., p. lvi.
16. Ibid., pp. 76-80.
17. Emergent norm theorists, Turner and Killian (1972: 5-6) specifically call for analysis at both levels, *Collective Behavior,* 2nd ed. (Prentice-Hall, Englewood Cliffs, N.J., 1972).
18. Ibid., p. 81.
19. Turner and Killian (1972), p. 5.
20. *The Official Report of the New York State Special Commission on Attica* (New York, Bantam Books, Photo No. 23, 1972).

CHAPTER 4

HOW FORM AFFECTS THE FUNCTIONS THAT PRODUCE IT

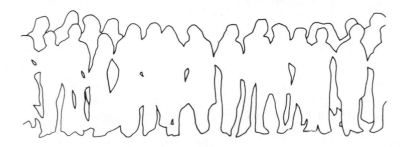

DESCRIPTIVE ACCOUNT #9: MILITARY GAMES[1]

It was an insufferably hot, humid and mosquito-laden Phillippine night. Just before lights out, the word began to circulate, accompanied by much excited moving about and raised voices, that some paratroopers had seriously beaten and injured a marine from the company in the barracks across the way. By the time the scratchy record of taps was finished playing over the P.A., some 150 to 200 of us were milling outside in the dark between the buildings. A couple of extremely angry friends of the injured man led us off towards the temporary billets of the airborne.

I do not believe any of us expected an organized reception party. But, as we crossed the open grass fields separating the units, the dark knot of men beside one of their buildings grew larger and larger, as the army poured outside. We came to a halt some 10 to 15 feet from their formation. I could see that, though many of them were in underwear, everyone was wearing combat boots — a sign that all were prepared for action.

The two task groups in this situation are engaged in interdependent activities. The actual interaction between the groups began at well over 100 yards. The direction of movement of the Marines was modified in response to the spotting of the cluster of paratroopers. The converging of more paratroopers was a reaction to the large mass of fast moving Marines closing the gap between the forms.

As the spatial distance between the groups narrowed, other reciprocal interactions occurred. The Marines began to move closer together increasing the density of their formation. The paratroopers began to collectively face the advancing form. They also extended the length of their own formation as many men moved to the outside ends of their group in order to be up front.

The interactions that were taking place changed as the spatial distances between the groups changed. Different distances produced different situational pragmatic problems which had to be dealt with. As a consequence, situational meanings, degrees of urgency, and proper body orientations changed as a function of the reduction of space between the group formation. The final stage of spatial reduction brought even more changes in the collective behaviors:

> It was clear that these men had been in similar situations in the past. While there was much calling out between them, as friends located friends in the dark, it was done in muted voices, so as not to bring down the M.P.'s. We had barely stopped and extended the width of our group to match that of the paratroopers, when one of the angry friends called across the space: (to paraphrase), "We want the shit-eating, dog-faced, motherfuckers who jumped Dan!"
>
> The reply was instantaneous and far more parsimonious: "Come and get 'em, Asshole!" At that moment, it was apparent to all that reasoned discourse had reached an impasse. To paraphrase C. Wright Mills — there are times when all other efforts have failed, when there is nothing left to do but beat one another over the head.
>
> No sooner had the response been uttered, than the angry friend, honing in on the army spokesman, crossed the space separating the two groups, and hit him with all the might that his anger, momentum and hardened muscles could manufacture. Most of the Marines had followed on his heels, closing the space between the groups and between knuckles and faces and knees and groins.

This chapter continues the discussion of group forms. Instead of looking at forms in and of themselves, if focuses on a product of forms. That is, the spaces that come to interactionally exist around forms and between them. These group spaces have been selected for analysis for two reasons.

First, they are an important aspect of collective interaction. The maintenance of a space around a group sets that group off from others in a situation. On this basis, it becomes possible to attribute social identity and form to the group. It also makes it possible to attribute the label "group" to collectivities. These and other functions of group space will be discussed throughout the chapter. Secondly, these spaces have independent effects within collective interactions. In this latter respect, they are of special interest to the argument as so far developed. While forms are dependent upon the collective activities that produce them, and the spaces about the forms are dependent upon the forms for their existence, these group spaces play an important and continuous role in all collective activities. This is one of the major ways in which forms affect the functions that produce them.

In the previous account, the closing distance or space between the approaching Marines and the paratroopers was associated with a rise in tension and preparation for conflict. The momentary 10 to 15 foot confrontation space took on special situated meaning. The crossing and the closing of this spatial gap became an infraction that signaled the start of the conflict. These group spaces came to have an independent effect in the collective interaction.

With the following account, we shall begin our analysis of group space. From this material, a definition of group space is developed. The nature of this space as a contour and as a negotiated realm is examined.

DESCRIPTIVE ACCOUNT #10: A STUDENT RIOT[2]

The eighteen policemen were formed on line, perpendicular to the building. The student demonstrators were surrounding them, except at the right end of the line which ended at the side of the building. Students in the front of the line were approximately five to six feet away from the baton-gripping, riot-dressed officers. The demonstrators at the exposed end of the formation were within a couple of feet of the end of the line. At first, students had closed in behind the officers' backs, also within a couple of feet. Then the Lieutenant in charge moved behind the formation, telling people to move back. They did so, but only a couple of feet, and this distance was halved when he returned to his command position.

The jointly developing literature on spatial use and behavior of animals — ethology — and the behavior of men in terms of their spatial relations — proxemics — has produced a set of observations and theories on personal space.[3] Drawing on this literature, Goffman offers the following definition of personal space:

The space surrounding an individual, anywhere within which an

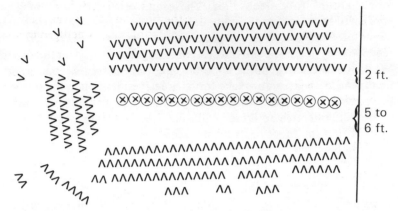

Figure 4.1 Stationary police/student confrontation showing group space and contour

entering other causes the individual to feel encroached upon, leading him to show displeasure and sometimes to withdraw.[4]

For lions, Hediger[5] notes that the boundaries of this space is determinable within inches. Stepping across this boundary and into the space produces an immediate volative reaction. For humans, Hall[6] suggests that there are four zones of spatial distances. The personal zone, most closely parallels social scientists and the ethologists' conception of the zone of personal space.

While these observations have been developed primarily in terms of individual animals and humans, similar behavioral spatial relationships appear around and between groups of humans in collective behavior situations. We will call this group space. The definition above can be useful to the understanding of group space, especially when a proviso is added. For the individual, "a contour, not a sphere is involved, the spatial demands directly in front of the face being larger than at the back."[7]

A contour is the shape or outer boundary of the personal space which has an irregular configuration. In the account so far, two aspects of the stationary contour of the group space of the police formation parallels that of the individual personal space. Police and students during the stationary period maintained an interactional distance that was approximately twice as much in the front of the formation as in the back, i.e., five to six feet in the front and two to three feet in the rear. In addition, the distance maintained to the side was as close as that to the rear and, at times, even closer. A contour of maintained group space surrounded the formation:

> After the usual illegal assembly notification, the Lieutenant in-structed his men, and so the confronting students. He told them to move in order to clear the area. When the officers stepped forward, in the initial hesitant steps of a guarded walk, reflecting concern with maintaining a uniform line, the normal pandemonium took place to the front of the line. This was characterized by a panicky flight of those in front to "get out of reach" of the now moving policemen. When a distance of approximately fifteen to twenty feet had been obtained, the confronting students turned and moved backwards at the same rate as the advancing officers. They continued to jeer, yell obscenities, and give off cries of, "Oink, oink, here come the Pigs." The space between the confronting students (density) was now much less than before when all were stationary.
>
> The interesting thing was the distance and behavior of those students to the side and rear of the policemen. As the officers moved forward, so did the students behind them — and at the same close distance as before. The space between the students themselves, in the rear, then widened. They became less compacted as the officers moved away and students moved at different rates in trying to keep up. This spread the students out over a wider area. Those viewing demonstrators to the side of the advancing sweep, stood calmly in their close distance to the police. They edged back only a little when the end of the formation actually came abreast of them. Then, the passed-by students would either join in behind or remain on the sidelines.
>
> The behavior of the students, immediately behind the officers, was that of cautionary movement — ready for retreat. Those further back were more bold and shouting derogatory comments and curses, as per their counterparts in front. Those standing to the side gave practically no aggressive signs of movement or shout. They had settled into viewing behavior.

In slow movement, the contour changed, in that the distance established in front of the formation tripled. The rear and side distances, in remaining the same during the movement, are indices of the importance of the relationship of the task, formation, and group space. When the officers reversed their field, the same group space and contour emerged.

The conclusion to be drawn is that the spatial form of the group becomes that organization around which a group space and contour emerges. This group space is similar in its front and rear contours to individual personal spaces. Two interactional variables appear to be significantly related to how the size and shape of the group space emerges. These are: (1) the direction in which the group is facing and acting (2) its rate of movement in that direction.

The fact that group forms can have a front, back, and sides affects whether other groups within the situation will be viewers or task oriented. Those people to the side will remain viewers throughout. Those to the front and rear alternate between being a task group and a viewing group as a function of the direction of movement of the police. The norms of appropriate behavior and role relation to the police vary according to group activities. At all times interactions are between these groups and not between individual police and individual students.

> When the Lieutenant saw that he was not clearing the area, because of the students following in behind, and those at the side simply not moving at all, he ordered his men to halt and to face about. At this point, the rioters who had been facing the rear of the formation, found that they were facing the police. These students then broke into the wild flight of disarray as they, also, sought to "get out of reach of." The rioters who had been facing the police, and now found themselves at their backs, proceeded to close into within two or three feet of the backs of the officers, as the other students had done when the formation was in the opposite direction. When the movement resumed, the students who were now facing the officers, moved further back and all was as before, i.e., a sweep was being made to no avail. This interaction sequence was repeated twice before reenforcements arrived. With more men available, the police frustration over the sweeping and clearing operations, entered a new phase.

Another proviso from Goffman can add further to our understanding:

> Indeed, in human studies, it is often best to consider personal space not as a permanently possessed, egocentric claim, but as a temporary, situational preserve in whose center the individual moves.[8]

In effect, what is being pointed to here is that group space is an interactional product. Its contour has an emergent and changing quality that is continually negotiated in and through interaction, within the limits of the shape of the form of which it is an extension. This form structures and limits what spatial distances will be put up for negotiation and the effective outcome on the contour.

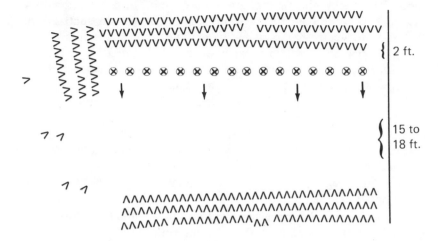

Figure 4.2 Moving police/student confrontation showing extended forward contour of the group space

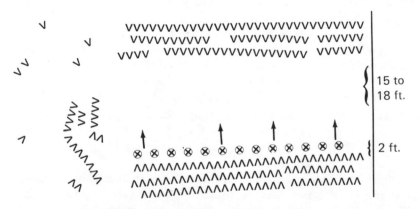

Figure 4.3 Reversed direction of movement by police/student confrontation showing how the extended contour is related to direction and movement

The Lieutenant's passage behind the line of his men was aimed at establishing a greater distance between the rear of the formation and the potential threat of the too-close demonstrators. He walked nervously, but with steady resolve, the full length, ordering people back. Yet, even with his physical presence, he had only limited success negotiating a new rear distance. When he returned to the focus of the formation, that small gain was greatly reduced. The negotiation for a new contour behind the ranks was not consistent with the spatial form that had emerged from the task at hand. The group space contours of that formation could not be changed drastically *without changing the formation itself.* That would have meant, changing the basic approach which was being used to carry out the task.

Nevertheless, the spatial contour was, to a degree, interactionally modified.[9] The number of demonstrators, the stage of the riot's development, the lack of back-up police on the scene, the unclear norms of violence that would emerge on both sides, etc., are all interactional factors that influence how the group space emerges in any point in time. Taking into consideration all of the above, a definition of group space can be offered.[10]

Group Space: The space surrounding a form which emerges out of interaction with others, such that the entering of the others into this space causes members to feel encroached upon, leading them to react frequently in terms of collective defense, attack, withdrawal, or disintegration. The contours of these group spaces are frequently irregular configurations.

Care must be taken to distinguish group form and group space from other kinds of territorial claims. Group form is that which is coterminous with the actual body distribution formation of a group. Group space is an empty area, a contour surrounding or extending out from this actual embodied configuration. These spaces, and claims made on their behalf, move about with the group and are dependent upon the group's continued existence. In effect, these are highly mobile territories subject to constant negotiational changes and to dissolution when the group disperses.

Other defensible spaces are based on a wider, more situationally fixed, territorial claim. That is, they are claims over a physical area wider than the group's spatial embodiment. As such, they are external and designatable independent from the group's form and contour. In this respect, a park or a street can become a situationally negotiated, fixed or located, territory.

In the riot account, we see how group form and group space are used in an attempt to interactionally negotiate wider territorial claims. When the officer in charge declared that an "illegal assembly" was occurring, he was also making the initial move to stake out a wider territory. The student response of derisive defiance — cheers and jeers and, most importantly, refusing to move out of the claimed area — set the stage for the attempted implementation of the territorial claim. Having announced that the students were now occupying a place illegally and having received an improper response, the police began their next move. This was to try to clear the claimed area. The sweep across a chosen area became, in effect, that territory which was to be understood as the area that the "illegal assembly" announcement was aimed at. The sweep was accomplished by moving the group, and with it, its group space forward. No physical contact was made with the demonstrators as they were moved back by the external contour of the police's group space. The irony was that the students in the rear also moved with the police. As a consequence an area was moved across, but the police ended up controlling no more space than they occupied with their embodied formation. They were also still totally surrounded by the demonstrators. The reversing of the ranks with a return sweep had the same null effect.

Though the territorial claim failed, the use made of the group space is informative. By moving slowly forward, instead of charging into the ranks of the demonstrators, the opportunity was given for the demonstrators to withdraw out of the extended group space. The students in effect, were being moved about, and interacted with, on the basis of the police's group space. The space became a resource used to clear an area nonviolently. The demonstrators also used the space by maintaining a close distance to the rear of the formation. But, this use, and the nonviolent possibilities that came out of it, are themselves dependent upon the group form of the police. Differences in this form result in different group spaces emerging. Different configurations of group space have different use possibilities. Note the following accounts.

DESCRIPTIVE ACCOUNT #11: THE CHICANO RIOT[11]

There were at least ten giant speakers on the Police sound truck. Yet even when the illegal assembly announcement was made at full volume, it could barely be heard from my central location among the 3,000 angry, shouting, and milling Chicano demonstrators (time: 3:57 p.m.)[12]

This actually made little difference, however, for at exactly 3:57.35, five files of riot-equipped officers entered the area. Even those demonstrators who might have wished to comply, were left with no time to do so.

The system and group perspective recommended in the last chapter is relevant here. Both news and police accounts located the cause of the ensuing 'riot' with the Chicanos. Some local politicians demanded a halt for further issuance of permits to demonstrate until Chicano leaders could assure control over their people. The assumption throughout these accounts being that the Chicano "crowd" lost control over itself and rioted.

In fact the demonstration had been totally under leadership and self-control, and it was scheduled with the police to end in three minutes. The initial trouble began when police ordered, via bullhorn, a viewer formation to "get off" the fence. Though they had been on the fence for an hour, compliance was immediate. Nevertheless, an illegal assembly was declared as advancing police broke-up the picketing task formation.

By these actions the police who had been viewers became task participants. Those who had been engaged in the task activity of picketing were forced back into a merger with viewers. At this point a new type of interdependent task activities emerged. These were social control activities of "riot activities." Neither the start of the riot nor what follows is understandable without considering the whole system of group relationships.

The objective consideration of all group interactions also adds to our understanding that there is no single causal process by which all riots start. I have seen riots start because police command wanted one, because protest leaders wanted one, because police command lost control over their men, because protest leaders lost control over their people, because tempers or fun and games escalated when no one wanted a riot, because a symbolic issue aroused so much emotion — frustration, etc. — among people that they engaged in this form of expression/action almost spontaneously, because of misunderstanding and lack of communication, and also from clear understanding and perfect communication.

This point is especially important to both lay and sociological crowd theorists. Explanations indicating the role of attitudes (prejudice), demographic factors (education levels, income levels), structural factors (degree of community organization), diffusion of ideology (Marxism or Christianity) are important as specifications of conditional variables. But these should not be confused with the interactional level where reality actually unfolds through processes of its own. Processes that are often strongly influenced by, but are operating independently of, the other factors.

The police approached the crowd in a manner I have never seen before. There were initially five separate files of 12 men each, with one group being approximately 500 feet in front of the others. By file, I mean that they were in single file, in a kind of safari fashion. The lead group was moving at a steady, almost full stride into the area. Two of the other groups actually broke into a trot, when the first file reached the crowd — apparently in an attempt to catch up.

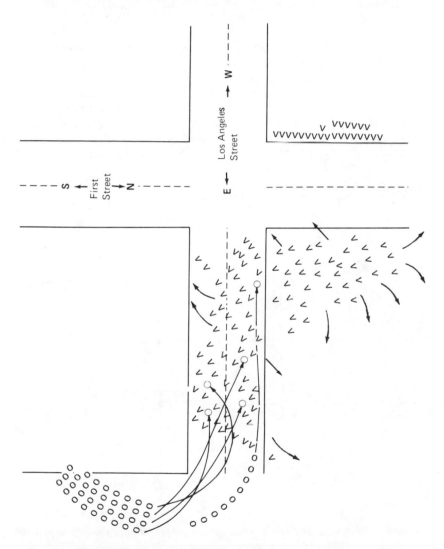

Figure 4.4   Five files of police cutting through protest formation causing its disintegration-flight behavior

They did more than that. Their momentum was such that they passed the first group and cut their way deep into the crowd. People began to flee in every direction. Many found themselves between the groups of officers (which were approximately 12 to 15 feet from one another) and some of these fell to the ground in an apparent swoon or shock of entrapment. Others who had been passed by at first, began to move in the direction of the remaining two files or columns of officers. But on perceiving the additional sets of police, there were many cries of dismay and bumping of people, as some stopped short and others ran into them. Those behind the first two groups of officers and between the oncoming ones, eventually began to run to each side then turn back up the street giving wide berth to the forward groups of officers.

This soon cleared the immediate area between the forward three files of officers and the rearward two files that were now trotting to catch up. It left at least one-fifth of the crowd behind the police ranks. The rear groups of police caught up with, and joined with the front groups of officers who were now moving forward at a steady walk. The five columns ultimately came abreast of one another with approximately six or seven feet between the columns.

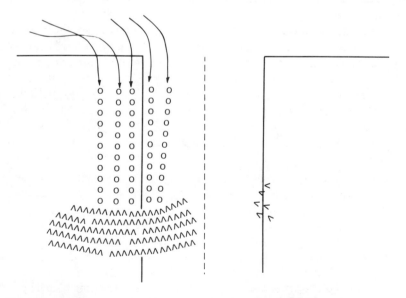

Figure 4.5 Police converge into military formation, rioters mass in response

The two variables initially stated to be important for the development of group space, are direction and speed and, by inference, time. In this account, the front direction of the single file formation was only one man in width. The unique spatial contour resulting was narrow, from side to side, with the distance between the formations varying from five to eight feet, depending upon how much lateral room could be granted the columns in the crunch of bodies.

For the trotting columns, forward contours extended out approximately ten to twelve feet. This was probably not their full length potential. The trotting columns would be hypothesized to have a greater forward contour than the walking ones. But the density of the crowd was such, that people could not see them coming until they were a short distance away. At that point, there would be frenzied movement to get to each side of the path of the onrushing police.

The point being that, under these conditions, the faster groups actually negotiated a shorter front contour than the slower ones. The slower columns allowed time for avoidance at an extended distance of approximately fifteen to eighteen feet. The faster files of officers simply could not provide sufficient time for such advanced avoidance to take place.

The spatial contours of these columns are affected by their speed and direction in yet another manner. A consistent direction of movement at a consistent speed becomes observable as a path. In the situation above, when paths became evident, the contours to the rear of the columns disappeared. People passed by or dodging the columns would run literally behind the last man in the files, sometimes just avoiding collision. The apparent commitment of the officers to a forward path, produced an effect of a less concern with the space left behind:

> The unification of the police in a common movement rate with a common front produced a solid thing that members of the crowd began to collectively react to. While most of the Chicanos continued down the street, a growing number of young kids, teenagers, young men, began to face the advancing police. They were moving backwards or sidestepping the police, keeping out in front of them at approximately 25 feet. Much angry verbal attack was directed at the officers — though many of the kids were jumping about, laughing and more or less enjoying a running game of "chicken" or "catch me if you can."
>
> The first bottle came hurtling out of the ranks of those behind the kids and young men. A short flurry of airborne missiles followed this bottle's

crash. The police stopped their forward momentum and newspapermen and cameramen who had been parallelling the police movement, quickly separated themselves from the vicinity. The nearest rioters were now 50 to 70 feet away — just at a good throwing distance. It only took a few moments of this before the police charged into the massed and stationary crowd that had come to face them. At first, they moved in their single file lines, breaking up the larger unit that they had previously been in. But as the distance was closed with the crowd, the single file lines broke down and the last few feet were closed with the rush of officers moving and swinging their clubs in every direction. Incredible as it may seem, this was the first physically violent contact made between the police and the demonstrators up to this point.

The front rank of the massed demonstrators tried to move back away from the charge but they were piling into one another and getting nowhere, as the middle ranks were not reacting as quickly, leaving the front ranks trapped. It was only when the officers began to penetrate into the crowds that the rear ranks of the crowds collectively took flight, leaving room for a general exodus.

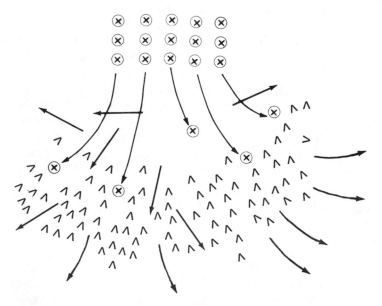

Figure 4.6   Police formation breaks down as individual officers cut into mass of rioters

There were three phases of police formation and group space used. One, when five single-file lines approached and entered the crowd at different speeds, places, times, and angles, pandemonium broke loose. Panicky movement to gain a distance outside the group space of the moving officers is a normal crowd reaction. But this situation had a compounding complexity. People frequently found (1) that they were unable to get far enough out in front of the trotting officers, (2) that the avoidance of one group put them in the path of another, (3) that they were caught between groups of officers, and (4) that they were passed by the officers and were put in the position of having to get around them in order to avoid being trapped behind them.

For many crowd members, the situation was one of terror and wild flight. At first, there was essentially not a visible or predictably safe place to be. The narrow files and forward movement produced extended group spaces which cut or sliced through the crowd. When done in the above manner, it produced total disorganization of protester and viewer activities. It further made it difficult for alternative organization to emerge as there was no focus to organize toward and react against.

When the five police columns converged, even though they were still moving, a broad front formation was established. This provided a single collective entity against which a collective response could be organized. While the police were still moving through the area, it was now in a sweep. The broad part produced a broad front contour outside of which and against which crowd member could organize a resistant reaction.

One must conclude that the broad formation has a group space contour that interactionally becomes the focus that attracts people to its front. This is in contrast to cutting through them.

The final phase was the police charge into that part of the crowd which had reassembled just outside their massed formation. Again, the basis of spatial relations was changed. When the charge disintegrated into individual actions, the only remaining contours to be interacted with in the situation became those of the individual policemen. This was so, even though the number of police and the individual spatial areas that they occupied did not change. When the officers broke down to individual acting units, the group space literally disappeared altogether. Individuals' personal space took over. Though these varied with the movement rates of each officer, they were, in comparison with the group contours, much shorter indeed.

The crowd reacted accordingly. At first the column movement caused a stir throughout the facing demonstrators. When the officers began acting individually, the back ranks of the crowd, having 40 to 50 people between them and the police, actually began engaging in viewing behavior of the activities in the front ranks. It took a physical pressure from those trying to flee, coupled with the advancing of some of the officers towards the back, to finally get those in back to turn and run.

In conclusion, different formations of police were able to negotiate different frontal group contours. Individual police personal space did not carry the same interactional power. The mass formation could move back masses of people, the file or column could part paths through the hearts of the crowd, the same number of individual acting officers had to negotiate individual personal spaces, and so lost the power of the collective form.

WHY AND HOW GROUP SPACES EMERGE

Defining group space as an interactional product (and not as an instinctual or ecological one) leads us to the consideration of social factors that support the emergence of the spaces. Some of these factors are outlined below in terms of recurrent problems that groups encounter in collective assembly situations. Group spaces are seen as emerging out of these practical contingencies of our material embodiment.

I. GROUP INTEGRITY

Defense or External Threat Reaction. Defense has become a sine qua non of personal space definitions.[13] Behavioral reactions by animals, to the distance-closing approaches of others, are taken as indicators that those being encroached upon interpret this closing as a threat. It is suggested that for groups of humans, similar spatial distance closings are equally crucial factors in interpretation processes which lend to the defining of spatial relations as threatening or not.

1. *Perception.* Keeping one's potential aggressor in sight is instrumental in defending one's self from surprise attack. In turn, keeping a potential enemy in sight is contingent on keeping him at a distance, i.e., out of reach. Through a series of fascinating photographs, Hall has

demonstrated that, for humans, a maintained distance of from seven to twelve feet is necessary in order to "see" the other — in his head-to-foot totality.[14] If the person moves within a closer range than the seven to twelve feet, then parts of him will continually be out of focus of the eyes. As a consequence, parts of the other at close distances can be used to launch a surprise attack, e.g., a knee in the groin.

Conclusion: keeping others at a distance in a potentially dangerous situation is necessary for visual control over the situation. Movement of others within this distance will be experienced as threatening and as a sign of confrontation.

2. *Time for Mobilization for Action.* Keeping others at a distance also creates a "buffer zone" or space which takes time for others to cross — if they are to aggress. This time passage allows the group the opportunity to mobilize for action. This is particularly important in group relations, because it gives the group time for coordinating and organizing a collective response. A collectivity which fails to maintain a group spatial zone can be readily fragmented and so disorganized by a sneak attack.

By definition, time, distance, and speed are intrinsically intertwined, speed being the length of the distance covered in a specific amount of time.[15] It is suggested here that this is one of the reasons that contours have more extended forward distances in moving versus stationary situations. When a group is moving towards another group, it decreases the amount of time that the other has for mobilizing a defense. This translates into a need to extend the contour distance interactionally according to the rate of approach of the potential invader.

Conclusion: Contour distances, and so defense reactions, are an interactional product of rates of closure as a reaction to the potential threat of not having enough time to prepare a defense.

3. *Gestures.* Reactions to movement and rates of closing distances are determined by more than just the time needs in a situation. Movement is not simply reacted to in a reflex manner. There is an interpretive relation between those being moved in upon and those moving. Meaning is being given to the movement by the potentially threatened.

Blumer notes that nonverbal actions can be interpreted as significant gestures, as elements in symbolic interaction. A gesture is, "any part or aspect of an ongoing action that signifies the larger act of which it is a part." Gestures "convey to the person who recognizes them an idea of the intention and plan of forthcoming action of the individual who presents them."[16]

How movements are interpreted becomes a fundamental factor in the decision on how to react to them. This understanding provides us with the insight that at times it is not the closing of distance, per se, that will be reacted to. Instead, reaction will be in terms of the meanings imputed to the various rates of closing distance. Therefore, contours will be negotiated as much by the rate of closure as by the amount of closure.

Tentative statements pertaining to these interpretations can be made: (1) The more rapid the movement of closing, the more likely it will be interpreted as a gesture of aggression; (2) The slower the closing of a distance, the less likely it will be interpreted as a gesture of aggression.

4. *Room for Movement.* The spatial contour around a group becomes in effect the walls of a room in which intragroup movements occur. The contours provide a boundary within which members can move about. This is particularly important for those movements necessary to put up a defense. Thus, even when totally surrounded by others, the helplessness of entrapment is avoided if the integrity of the contour is maintained.

The reduction of the "room" or contour brings about a crowding or a consequent loss of mobility. This increases the threat in the situation as it leaves less room for the internal movements necessary in order to mobilize for defense. It thereby increases the urgency of the need for action. Therefore, groups and individuals react to invasion of their spatial contours in anticipation of the danger of immobilization.

Where an intragroup movement is necessary in order to prepare for defense, the closing in on the group's contour leads to a defensive reactions, because it threatens the conditions for the intragroup movement necessary for its survival.

5. *Sanctuary.* The group and its contour become an area that is bigger than the individual can claim and maintain by himself. Therefore, the contour of the group can become a sanctuary that individuals will seek in the middle of a conflict. In the next account, many of the functions of group space, as discussed above, are in operation. These will be pointed out in some brief comments following the depiction of the deceitful events at the "Love-In."

DESCRIPTIVE ACCOUNT #12: LOVE-IN[17]

What was to be a rock concert, be-in, and a time for good vibes, had long since turned into fun and games of a different kind. The weekly police harassment of the Sunday Love-In at the Park's Merry-go-round area had evolved into a confrontation.

The police have been standing in a long line facing us for about five minutes.

A second illegal assembly announcement is being made.

People are spread out at various distances and angles from the row of officers. Most had stopped their fleeing when the police sweep had stopped.

It is a beautiful day and now the long hairs are sitting or standing in small groups, casually talking, relaxing throughout the area.

Just enough attention seems to be directed to the officers to make situational status checks. The officers are relaxed, as well. Some have lit cigarettes; many have secured their nightsticks to their belts.

These "time outs" from collective activities and collective focused orientations, are a common feature of collective assemblies. "Time out" *norms* accompany these activity changes. When marching bands in the Rose Parade would come to a rest halt, members would begin talking among themselves and to audience members. Milling behavior dominates the collective activities between acts of play. In riots I have seen officers and rioters, who before had been in confrontation, exchange cigarettes and conversation. Later these same people would resume passioned and violent exchanges.

The edge of the collectivity nearest the officers is approximately 20 to 25 feet from them. A red-headed officer near the middle of the line has become noticeable as he begins to make beckoning signals to someone near the edge of the collective formation.

A young fellow in a doctors'-type smock has finally responded with a pantomimed set of his own gestures. With a broad sweep of his arm, he pointed to himself as he mouthed the question, "Who, me?"

The vigorous affirmative head-nodding of the officer is accompanied by an extension of his right arm towards the man while the index finger moved back and forth in request that he "come here."

The young man simply looks perplexed at the request and stands in his place.

The officer's reaction was that of impatience. He raised both his hands in front of himself, to show that they were empty, then he extended his arms (as on a cross) to both sides of himself, calling attention to the "time out from serious interaction" attitude that the row of officers was engaged in.

Manifesting embarrassment at being publicly inconsiderate to a personal request for communication/help, the young man picked up a white case with a red cross painted on the sides and took a few hesitant steps out into the spatial no-man's land between officers and "rioters."

At this hesitating, the officer showed more impatience and hurt/disgust that this guy would not trust his good will in such a public forum. He languidly, with exaggerated motion, pulled his arm from in front of himself to his chest.

The symbolic pulling was successful. The white smock moved slowly towards the police line.

By this time, a good proportion of the rioters are viewing the unfolding tableau with interest but with no apparent alarm or change of position. Many of the policemen also seemed to focus on this man all alone crossing the buffer zone.

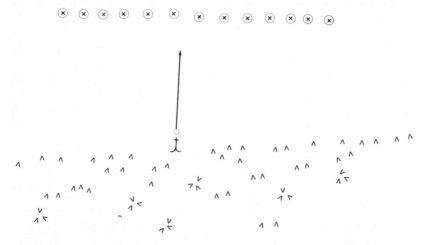

Figure 4.7 Deceit at the love-in

The manner in which the medic approached the police line was interpreted as nonthreatening. Though the distance was closed, it was done slowly and nonaggressively. The line of officers unconcernedly watched. Later, when the whole group of rioters began a running charge towards the line, every officer crouched or otherwise braced himself. Different meanings were imputed to those different spatial closing gestures. Here it was primarily as a function of difference in the number and rate of speed of the rioters closing the space.

When he was three or four feet from the officer, the young man stopped and it appeared that he was asking the officer what he wanted.

The officer did not verbally reply, but made a further gesture that he come closer, seemingly so that they could talk without the other officers hearing.

The young man now gave off two sets of the most contradictory signs imaginable. He ever so slowly continued his movement — as if not wanting to look foolishly like someone who could not make up his mind to complete an act once it was embarked upon. At the same time, his body demeanor reflected total distrust and fatalistic resignation to the possibility of having over committed himself to a course of action that he could not get out of. The inability of the officer to provide a legitimate reason for having called him over there was determined too late.

The closing of distance reduced the time that the medic could have used for mobilization of flight or fight behavior. His final hesitation, prior to coming into arm's reach of the officer, was in recognition that in a few more feet, he would be out of the time needed to carry out defensive actions.

When the young medic crossed through the group space, he paid the price of not maintaining sufficient distance for perceptual control of the situation. The closer he got to the officer, the less able he was to see and to anticipate any sudden movements on behalf of the officer. As a consequence, it became an embarrassingly simple act for the officer to reach out and grab the "rioter."

As soon as the young man was within arm's length, the red-headed officer grabbed him by the front of his smock and jerked him across the remaining distance. The white medical case went flying through the air opening upon impact, spilling its contents upon the green grass.

I have never before heard such a simultaneously collective and immediate cry of infuriated disbelief come from such a large number of people. From all over the area, people were jumping to their feet and running, yelling, at the officers.

The struggling young man was falling to the ground (resisting arrest) when an officer, next to the red-headed one, turned and repeatedly rammed his nite-stick into his writhing body. Another officer, three or four places down the line, broke rank and joined in the clubbing.

The noise from the closing rioters became a genuine "collective howl of outrage."

I could hardly believe what I had seen or what I was seeing. The row of officers braced for the impact of a charging mass, when deux ex machina, another group of police entered the scene (evidently these were reenforcements that the first group had been waiting for). This increased the amount and volume of yelling even more than before. It also stopped the charge of the rioters. After a brief red-faced yelling confrontation across five feet of space, the rioters, minus one, again fled as all the officers began to advance.

One final point, when the medic crossed the space, he did more than move into striking distance of the officers. He also gave up the sanctuary that existed on the rioters side of the group space. By leaving that collectively established sanctuary, he took a risk in personal negotiation of self-defense. In hindsight, it was a risk that seems to have been based more on romantic thinking than on Machiavellian logic.

II. SOLIDARITY — INTERNAL NEEDS

Group space contours emerge for internal solidarity needs — as well as for defensive needs. The continuation of the group (under conditions necessary for carrying out its activities) depends on a contour maintenance in the interactional setting. Groups need and use group space contours for the following internal solidarity reasons.

Boundary Maintenance and Identity. The continued practical functioning of groups depend on their maintenance of an interactional identity. Group contours help maintain identity in several ways.

1. When there is no clear-cut sign in a situation by which membership can be read, then spatial segregation can serve this identification need. Those within a contour belong to one group; those outside it belong to other entities. The spatial buffer of the contour becomes a boundary supporting this identity. For example, parades in many cities are often patroled by motorcycle officers. They ride up and down the edge of the audience form keeping audience members from intermixing with the paraders. The police, in effect, are outriders who maintain spatial buffers and form boundaries.

2. Even when there are other signs of membership available in a situation, e.g., uniforms, group contours serve as an ordering device to distinguish between those who are to act in a certain manner from others in the situation, e.g., police who are going to sweep an area versus those who are going to stand guard over equipment. Here the contour surrounding, and identifying membership in different task activity groups, serves as a basis for distinguishing how various members are committed to act at this particular time.

MEMBERSHIP MAINTENANCE AND COMMITMENT.

1. *Membership loss.* Membership loss is inhibited by group space. The movement out of the group becomes a visible act by reason of having to cross the open space. The resulting cost of being exposed to labeling as a defector and the derision in the situation itself become a conciously manipulated factor. This is reflected in leaders' attempts to keep outsiders away from their group, even in nonconfrontation situations. The loss of membership and group identity due to fusion and intermingling of the active group with viewer groups is a constant problem to leaders at rallies. Their calls for actions often fail under these conditions as lazy members find anonymity in the undifferentiated viewer-task formation.

2. *Membership Gain.* Membership gain is at times dramatized by the creation of a contour or the crossing of one. The cry of "Where do you stand?" can lead to commitment crises during a mutiny. Undecided members or those wishing to go over to the other side, must cross the space between the groups. The spatial contours, then, not only keep the groups apart from one another, but the very crossing of a space to join a group can become an initiation rite of immense proportion.[18]

III. FUNCTIONAL NEEDS.

As so far indicated, group contours have come into being and continue to exist for a variety of interactional reasons. As mentioned earlier, not the least of these is their use value in a situation. Suggested below are interactional factors (nonconfrontational situations) out of which group spaces emerge. They are created or appear in order to meet a practical contingency in the situation.

1. *Working Space.* Focused gatherings are distinguished by a division of labor in space. By definition, there are always those who are doing some activity and those who are watching. In all but exceptional circumstances — e.g., when four thousand people try to storm a building — there is a negotiated spatial contour around the actives separating them from the viewers. At an accident scene, the call automatically goes out for, "Give us room" or "Move back! Give him air!" A contour is being negotiated around the actives with the watchers on the outside perimeters of it. This keeps the viewers out of the way of the actives.

2. *Viewing Space.* More formally focused gatherings maintain a contour about the actives in order to establish a distance so that people

cannot get so close as to block the views of those behind. This is readily visible as the zone between the stage area and the audience. News-papermen and cameramen frequently claim an exemption status and move about at will within this group spatial zone.

3. *Buffer Space.* Group spaces emerge and are shaped by the movement needs of the group as a whole. Whenever the group is moving from point A to point B, there is always the need to maintain a path. This path is a negotiated spatial contour which serves as a buffer zone. The laws of physics require that clusters of particles be segregated from other particles moving at different rates of speed if friction is to be avoided and unimpeded flow is to occur. Group spaces serve this buffer function.

In this chapter, we have reversed the question guiding Chapter 2 and Chapter 3. Here we have considered one of the ways that group forms can affect group functions. The space that comes to surround a collectivity in interaction is seen to be dependent on the form which the collectivity manifests. In turn, this group space becomes a major factor influencing how the interactions of the collectivities are carried out. In this manner, we have looked at how form affects function.

This completes our elaborations on the group form-function relation-ship. The centralness of form to collective interaction, and the complexity of the compounding roles that forms have in these interactions, of necessity has kept the analysis limited. But now sufficient basic knowledge has been established to permit the ad-dressing of the original question we set out to consider. What can an analysis of form contribute to solving that most important and historically perplexing of problems — how does collective coordina-tion of activities occur in collective behavior?

NOTES

1. From the repertoire of personal adventures of Sam Wright (1963).

2. Sam Wright, Field Notes. Student/Police confrontation during the protest over the invasion of Cambodia (May 11, 1970).

3. For example, see H. Hediger, *Studies of the Psychology and Behavior of Captive Animals in Zoos and Circuses* (London: Butterworth Scientific Publica-tions, 1955), pp. 40-42; Edward T. Hall, *The Silent Language* (New York: A Fawcett Premier Book, 1959).

4. Erving Goffman, *Relations in Public* (New York: Harper Colophon Books, 1972), pp. 29-30.

5. H. Hediger (1955), pp. 40-42. Fight or Flight behavior as a function of critical distance.

6. Edward T. Hall, *The Hidden Dimension* (New York: Doubleday-Anchor Books, 1966), pp. 113-130.

7. Erving Goffman (1972), p. 30.

8. Ibid., p. 31.

9. Despite his obvious interactionist approach, Goffman's definition does not incorporate the interactional basis for personal space emergence. Personal space appears as a given area about the individual. Most ethologists give little attention to the interactional determinants of the personal space. Instincts are assumed to be the foundational bases.

10. In modification of Goffman's initial statement.

11. Sam Wright, Field Notes (January 9, 1971).

12. Illegal assembly announcements are not automatic commitments by the police to clear the area. There is no law-being-broken normative demand that they do so. Instead, the announcement in practice is a strategy ploy in situation. If the people have an obedience response, so much the better. If not, then frequently the police ignore their own declaration and try other moves, such as negotiation with leaders.

In any case, it is an act that can be pointed to in future situations, where the police are being held accountable (a legitimizing account to justify their actions as being necessary) for their actions. If confrontation develops, the nonpolice are automatically at fault for having been illegally in the situation, if the police have properly covered themselves first by declaring an illegal assembly.

As a consequence of knowing this, police use "illegal assembly" declarations frequently disregarding any consideration of whether there is law-breaking going on or potential law-breaking in the situation.

Essentially, this gives the police the power to make any ongoing collectivity illegal.

13. Goffman's definition is typical in this feature.

14. Edward Hall (1966), p. 127.

15. Jean Piaget, *The Child's Conception of Time* (New York: Ballantine Books, 1971), p. 29.

16. Herbert Blumer, *Symbolic Interactionism: Perspective and Method* (Englewood Cliffs, N.J.: Prentice-Hall, Inc., 1969), p. 9.

17. Sam Wright, Field Notes (1970).

18. Winston Churchill, in noting the function of having the two parties in the House of Commons facing one another across a buffer space — the Floor — says in reference to changing parties "the act of crossing the Floor is one which requires serious considerations" and "it is a difficult process." Leonard Broom and Philip Selznick, *Sociology,* 5th ed. (New York: Harper and Row Publishers, 1973), pp. 240-241.

CHAPTER 5

GROUP FORM
AND NONVERBAL COMMUNICATION

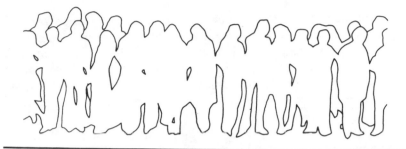

Actors in collective behavior situations are engaged in interpretive processes. But, unlike small group interactions, verbal input into the interpretive processes is frequently minimal or even nonexistent. Verbal discussions of alternatives of actions, of what norms to follow, of the consequences of the actions to be taken, often cannot be aired and negotiated in the midst of crowd interactions. Therefore, this normal source of input into a situation, and its social control implications is absent.

When verbal interaction of this type does occur, it is among dozens, even hundreds, of small groups. But actions in these situations are collective and not small group. Not knowing how other individuals and small groups have interpreted the situation, inevitably forces people to turn to the situation itself as an information resource. As a consequence, actors must rely on what they *perceive* in a situation, i.e., what is available to be *read out of it* through direct perception. There is no other mechanism continually and jointly available for the coordination of their behavior.

Interaction emerging under these circumstances is largely dependent upon the immediate behavioral cues of others in the situation. In this sense, crowds are, indeed, less institutionalized, patterned, or organized than small groups under more normal circumstances. Yet these situations are not a social vacuum that irrationality rushes in to fill. There is order and meaning to be perceived in the behavior of others. And a major source of these meaningful behavioral cues is the spatial relations of the member and the group forms that emerge from their collective activities.

The present chapter continues with the analysis of group forms. The primary focus will be to explicate what has been an underlying assumption in the preceding discussion. That is, group forms are not only a product of collective interaction, but they also serve as a medium of *nonverbal communication* in those interactions. As such, group forms are instrumental to the coordination of activities in collective assemblies.

It is not surprising that spatial forms are major elements of communication in crowd settings. Exposure to, and involvement in typically recurring task and crowd activities provide people with ample experience in associating or understanding which typical form emerges out of which typical activity. As a consequence, forms become an independent source of knowledge which can be read for cues as to what activities are unfolding. Once one can associate a type of spatial pattern as being a manifestation of a type of activity, then a newcomer to a setting can read out from the empirically available form what activity is occurring.

Members of ongoing collective assemblies also garnish information from changes in forms. The appearance of a new form, or the alteration of an old one, becomes immediate focuses of collective attention. The new spatial patterns are read to determine what new emergent activities are thereby represented. People make assessments as to whether or not present activities are viable any longer, on the basis of the evaluation of the degree of present form disintegration or the attractiveness or disruptive potential of the activity the new form might represent.

The following nude beach affair is an exemplary depiction of the working of many of these processes. During this confrontation, nonverbal communication via form reading is the primary source of information that members must rely on throughout the event. It is worth noting that despite the aroused emotions in the situation, the collective behaviors are not simply irrational or imitative. Despite the lack of verbal keynoting, coordination of the collective behavior takes place and is appropriately adjusted to the changing problems encountered over the course of the collective interactions.

DESCRIPTIVE ACCOUNT #13: THE NUDE BEACH AFFAIR[1]

Background: For several weeks, the news media had been ballyhooing the remarkable developments at the Venice Beach. A segment of this beach had, for many years, been a place where locals did their sunbathing in the nude. But a recent mass invasion by outsiders had turned what was an unnoticed, semi-private activity into a yellow journalism public issue.

While the Roman Catholic Church and the Police were openly expressing disapproval, the city attorney stated that the law, as it presently stood, did not prohibit "nonlurid nudity"; i.e., nude bathing was legal. Legally limited, but not morally daunted, the police began to "make its presence felt on the beach" by having teams of officers, on foot, patrol it. Dressed in Bermuda shorts (color: Police blue) with pistols, handcuffs, nightsticks, ticket books, two-way radios and sunglasses, the officers, for days, had been issuing "warning" tickets, taking names, arguing with people to put on their swimsuits, and, in general, attempting to harass the bathers as acts of moral entrepreneurship. (To me, these were familiar signs of a confrontation situation in the making.)

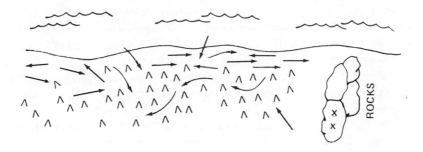

Figure 5.1 Nude beach scene
Key to symbols used: ∧ nude bathers; → voyeurs and exhibitionists; × police

As I approached the two hundred yard strip of beach, which the nude bathers had come to dominate, I was again struck by the density of the bathers here versus the other sections of the beach. Groups of bathers in the nonnude area had spatial distances between them of from eight to ten feet and up to fifty feet between them, forty yards from the shore. They were also spread out over the whole area of the wide beach, with only about one-half being within the twenty yards nearest the water.

In contrast, in the nude beach area, nine-tenths of the 3 to 4,000 bathers were within the twenty yards nearest the water. The spatial distances between groups of bathers varied from a couple of feet to barely any separation at all. To find a spot for oneself involved a careful picking of one's way through the densely packed bodies. I was reminded of the observation reported by Sommer[2] that people stood much closer together while waiting in line for an "X-rated movie," than for a Disney-type movie. Social binding, seeking of anonymity in a crowd, "we feelings," and a dozen other explanations came to mind as logical accounts for this density.

The perception of differences between the group forms became the basis for interpretation and action. The wide spread and diffused form appeared to be a normal configuration. By nonverbally reading (interpreting) the forms, one was seen as being normal, while the densely packed form required closer inspection before an interpretation could be made.

The form manifested at the nude beach was solid and compact. The sense of being set off from the rest of the areas was heightened by clear boundaries to the form. A group space surrounding the form added to its separate appearance. The crossing of this space gave one the definite feeling of joining a group.

Approximately half of the people on the beach were lying down. About one-quarter were sitting upright. The remaining one-quarter were either moving from the water to their places in the sand, swimming in the water, or promenading along the water's edge. Though there were many people who had come individually, approximately three-fifths of the bathers were made up of groups of from three to eight people. It was Saturday at mid-day and more people were entering the area than were leaving it.

Reading out of a form involves the reading of a configuration and the individual orientations of its members, in order to determine what collective activities they are engaged in. The primary collective activities taking place at this beach were: sunbathing, enjoying the water, and voyeurism/exhibitionism. People were distributed in space accordingly. The sunbathers were either sitting or prone, producing a long narrow formation twenty yards wide by several hundred yards in length near the water's edge. Those enjoying the water were either standing or swimming in it, or wading in the surf at the water's edge. They produced a parallel and adjacent formation to the sunbathers, full of much movement and far less densely packed. The overt voyeurs walked slowly through the sunbathers or along the water's edge — more or less openly staring. The exhibitionists followed the same pattern, but rather than staring, they were promenading.

> The first indication that something was amiss came after an hour and a half of sunbathing. From far off, the sounds of angry yelling and shouting reached my location. This was immediately followed by one-third of those in my area, jumping to their feet and looking in the direction of these unusual sounds. A hundred yards north of my location, there was a moving mass of nude bathers, parallel with and trailing behind two policemen who had two Black teenagers in tow. The police were walking hurriedly, and the 200 to 250 people strung out behind them, were trying to keep pace as they yelled in protest. From my area, and from the area between us and the police, and the area further South, people began to run towards this emergent focus. This convergent running involved about one-fifth of the sunbathers. Of these runners, approximately two-thirds were male.

> The police were moving towards a four-wheel drive jeep parked on the sand, some distance from the shoreline. The converging runners were moving in anticipation toward this vehicle rather than toward the police and their pursuers, per se. We all met there. It was indeed, a bizarre sight to behold.

The appearance of another collective form in this setting was, in and of itself, cause for attention. At a minimum this new form communicated the fact that an out of the ordinary and new activity was emerging. For those of us outside the emergent form a major problem in interpretation of the situation was precipitated by the presence of

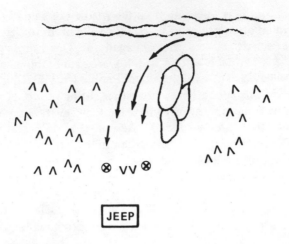

Figure 5.2 First emergent form: pursuit

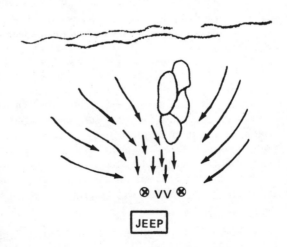

Figure 5.3 Second emergent form: pursuit plus convergence

this unusual distribution of people in space. The basic question to be answered was: What were people doing in this situation? Reading out of a form becomes instrumentally related to this. When I first observed the source of the yelling,[3] I observed a collectivity of people:

1. focusing on the same object, i.e., the officers and the two Blacks;

2. pursuing the focus in an elongated strung-out mass, and jeering and booing.

3. making gestures at the focus. These activities were actually there to be perceived or *read out of* the situation. This information was communicated nonverbally, i.e., without benefit of, or need for conversations with or from others.

What has been described to this point is the emergence of a form led by the police and their two captives. When people from all sections of the beach began to run towards this form, a second emergent form developed. This was a converging movement of people from different parts of the beach towards the jeep. This collective converging activity was likewise there to be *read out of* the collective form.

Some three hundred totally nude people were gathered in a large circle around the vehicle. More were arriving every second. The circle itself surrounded the jeep, but the encircling group was not pressed tightly in or about the vehicle. There was an open space of approximately twenty-five feet between the inside edge of the encircling demonstrators and the jeep itself. The police had the jeep's engine running, but did not try to break out. The situation remained in this manner for about a minute, then the encircling people began to slowly edge forward while yelling louder and louder. This moving forward was also reducing the space between the officers and the crowd. At this point, the driver of the jeep simultaneously raced the engine with a roar, turned on his siren, and began tapping a tatoo on the vehicle's horn. In the startled silence, the enclosing movement stopped. The jeep then shot forward spinning out a tail of sand from behind its rear wheels. With scattered yells of warning, "Look out," the circle opened in front of the moving machine. As the jeep passed on down the beach, there was a round of broken applause, plus laughter, many cat calls, and derogatory cries of "Oink, oink." In less than a minute, most of the people had left the area and returned to their places of sun worship and display.

During this time, I asked half a dozen people what the incident was all about and none had the slightest idea. I could hear others making the same inquiry and getting the same basic results. No one seemed to know why the Blacks were arrested, or if the arrest had anything to do with

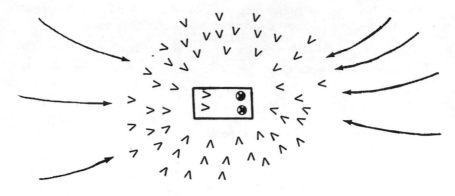

Figure 5.4 Bathers surround police jeep

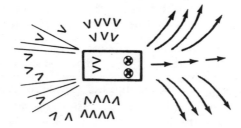

Figure 5.5 Police vehicle egress

nude sunbathing. By all appearances, it did not. Both of them were wearing surfer cutoffs.

At no time during this incident, did anyone give commands, verbally keynoting or assuming leadership. The individual to individual and individual to form relationships were coordinated on the basis of the reading out of the activities and forms of the fellow actors, what was going on and why. The practical problems encountered in pursuing these activities also led people to perceive what changes in activities were required in the situation. Thus, upon reaching the jeep, there was an immediate circling and an entrapment of it. This change of activity, and the subsequent closing in on the jeep, occurred without verbal direction.

As discussed in the introductory chapter, contemporary theories of collective behavior either fail to deal with nonverbal communication at

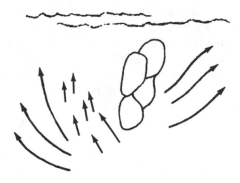

Figure 5.6 Crowd divergence

all, or treat it as an unreasoned imitation or contagion reaction to others. Yet, it is important to recognize the need for, and the importance of, form reading. The significant addition to the theoretical understanding of collective behavior which form reading can provide can be readily assessed by examining the shortcomings of what present theories have to say about communication in crowd behavior.

CONTEMPORARY THEORETICAL POSITIONS ON COMMUNICATION AND CROWD BEHAVIOR

As elaborated on in Chapter 1, it was suggested that three basic theoretical approaches have been used to explain crowd behavior.[4] These are: the emergent norm approach, the convergent approach, and the contagion approach. Each approach, in turn, assumes that communication and coordination in crowds occur through processes uniquely consistent with the assumptions of its own definition of how crowds function.

1. *The emergent norm position,* as expressed by Turner and Killian[5] emphasized the role of rumor in crowds.[6] Rumors are seen as constantly ongoing and emerging definitions of the situation. Changes in the activities of a group are held to stem from changes in the rumor-carried definitions of the situation. Throughout their discussion, verbal communications are stressed as being essential to collective actions, particularly changing actions. Their basic assumption is that

people act in a situation in terms of their definitions of that situation and that a change in people's activities must be accompanied by a change in their definition of a situation. Thus, it follows that if a collectivity changes its activities in a coordinated manner, then there must have been some collective verbal redefinition of the situation that took place. Rumor is seen as the medium through which collective definitions are transmitted in crowd behavior.

But rumors cannot account for changes in activities under all crowd conditions. Situations where there are thousands of people, spread out over a large area, and where the people change their activities several times within the course of minutes, are difficult to explain in terms of changing verbal definitions of the situation. The amount of time needed for rumor transmission, in and of itself, makes this a questionable explanation for how people in the crowds are coordinating their activities.

The account given before stands in contradiction to the emergent norm approach. The absence of rumor or even keynoting of verbal cries, such as "Get them!" or "Surround the jeep!" was particularly noted. Nevertheless, coordinated activities took place and changed over time.

2. *Convergent approaches,* most frequently, have been used by psychologists and sociologists who locate attitudes as the main determinants of actions. The position taken is — people with similar attitudes and predispositions to act in similar manners converge into a setting.[7] When something significant occurs, these similarly predisposed people tend to react and to act in the same manner to the same stimulus. Therefore, attitudinal factors established prior to the situation provided for the coordination of the behavior in the situation.

Though there is no attitudinal data from the nude beach incident, several comments can still be made. There was a converging on this beach of people who were drawn by the central fact of nudity. This awkward-to-get-to section of sand had been one of the least used parts of the beach before public nudity became associated with it. At the time of the incident, it was by far one of the most heavily used areas.

But an attitudinal stance cannot account for "how" people came to communicate and coordinate their activities in the emergent situation at the beach. For, if there were consistency in attitudes, two crucial problems undermine the explanations: (1) Why did *only* one-fifth of the supposedly similar attitude-holding people, i.e., nude bathers, respond at all? If there were consistent attitudes, they were seemingly producing different behavioral responses; (2) How do attitudes account for the types of changes in activities that occurred in the situation? The people were not simply responding to the stimulus of the police, but were also initiating actions that required meeting practical problems at hand, such as encircling and closing in on the police.

3. The emphasis of *contagion approaches* in nonverbal communication is more compatible with the idea of reading spatial forms that is being developed here.[8] Nevertheless, there remain major differences. In attempts to deal with the facts that a coordination takes place in crowds without "talk," contagion theorists have suggested two processes through which this occurs.

Imitation emphasized the synchronization of behavior via people in a crowd copying one another's behavior. By stressing imitation, a means of nonverbal communication between crowd members, the shortcomings of the mechanical stimulus-response or convergence position are avoided.

The second major process suggested by contagion theorists is that of contagion, itself. Assuming that crowds are basically irrational, following heightened beliefs, and emotionally crazed, the nonverbal communication of emotion and irrational actions is held to operate through a process of contagion.

But imitation and contagion processes have come under heavy criticism in the collective behavior literature.[9] Both have problems in accounting for either the initiation or termination of any particular behavior. If people imitate one another, then it remains unexplained as to how the original behavior gets started and why; how does one behavior become selected for imitation over other behaviors, and most crucially, why and how does the one imitative behavior come to be dropped and another adopted?

Contagion has similar difficulties. Why and how does one emotion come to be communicated rather than another? Why and how does a change from happy excitement to an enraged anger take place? And, most importantly, how does the circle of emotional reaction and of never-ending imitation come to end once started? If there is a spiral of increasing reinforcement, what prevents all crowds from ultimately collapsing in an exhausted confusion of emotional excess?

The problems of contagion theory stem from its primary imagery of the mental state of crowd members. By insisting that crowd members are acting in a blind, follow-the-leader, herd-like manner, or acting solely emotionally, an irrational, nonreflexive, cognitive state is assumed. Yet, as stated by many observers, this does not empirically seem to be the case at all.[10] And as Turner and Killian recently stated:[11]

> When a person challenges the established dictates or is forced to act when cultural dictates are nonexistent, vague, or contradictory, his behavior becomes unpredictable to others about him, making him hard to deal with, and his fellows may find it difficult to understand his behavior. . . .
> To refer to this behavior as irrational or emotional is either fallacious or tautological.

This critique being developed can be summarized as follows. The imitation/contagion approach is strong in its recognition of the role that nonverbal communication plays in collective behavior situations. Its primary shortcomings lies in its equating of the nonverbal with the irrational. There is ample evidence that interpretive processes are involved in nonverbal communications.

The convergence position also makes a strong contribution to our understanding of collective interaction. In many situations there is a genuine convergence of people who share some type of common attribute. These can range from people having similar social interests (sports fans), to those with common attitudinal predispositions (antiwar protesters), to those sharing demographic characteristics (race in a ghetto).

But these commonalities are only tangentially related to the interactional processes that take place in collective assemblies. While convergence can speak to the roles that shared predispositions have in influencing unfolding collective interactions, it has little to say as to the nature of these interactions.

Finally, the emergent norm theorists best articulate the need to demystify the accounts of how the processes of collective interactions work. By pointing to the continuing dependence of collective actions on interpretive processes, other suggested processes, such as the group mind or emotional contagion, are shown to fail to account for the fact that collective decision making regularly occurs. But the reliance on verbal communication as the major mechanism for explaining coordination of collective activities misses completely the significant dependence of people in collective behavior situations on interpretive processes based on nonverbal communication.

In the remaining section of this chapter, four criteria which are involved in the processes of the reading out of forms are discussed. These are presented as further statements toward the understanding of how forms communicate. The suggestion here is that all three prior theoretical perspectives will benefit from the incorporation of these ideas on the role of nonverbal communication via form reading.

INTERPRETIVE PROCESSES AND FORM READING

There are several factors which are relevant to how forms communicate or, more precisely, how interpretive processes work, in regard to forms and communication. The following discussion looks at the processes of reading out of forms.

1. **Negative Knowledge.** All forms communicate negative knowledge. This is the important information as to what is *not* going on in a situation. Upon my arrival at the nude beach, it was clear from the reading of the *absence* of forms, that a large number of other activities were not taking place. The presence of the sunbathing, swimming, and the voyeur/exhibitionist forms, and only these forms, denied the existence of other collective activities taking place in this setting.

It is a thesis of this study that upon entering a new area, evaluations of what is taking place in large part, rest on negative knowledge. That is, people look about and conclude that, "nothing is happening" or that "nothing out of the ordinary is going on" — in short, that "everything is as it should be in this kind of routine situation."

The imagery of the manner in which people should be distributed in space, if anticipated activities are taking place, is compared to what is visually available. The lack of any conflict between the imagery and reality is understood in terms of this negative knowledge.

2. **Changing Form.** Whenever a collective form starts to go through any kind of alteration, people inside and outside the form react to this as a phenomenon warranting common focusing. This is particularly true when there is something special about the nature of the change. That is, it is unexpected; it has extraordinary significance; it is taking place for unknown reasons; it is out of phase of what should be happening; it is representative of some major breakdown in cooperative relations; it is threatening, interrupting, stopping the ongoing, etc.

Given the relation of form to activity, the focusing is not surprising. A change in a form is looked to as an indicator of an activity change, or at least, a challenge to the ongoing activities. It thus becomes not only a stimulus for the search for (or the imputation of) its meaning, but, also an impetus for people to change their own ongoing activities and converge towards the new point of focus. As the following account demonstrates, this can create a rapid dissolving of an existing form as members abandon it in order to "see" what is happening.

DESCRIPTIVE ACCOUNT #14:
THE JANE FONDA RALLY[12]

The turnout to this daytime antiwar rally was a moderate 1,000 to 1,200 people. By 2:30, an audience-speaker focus was well underway, with most of the millers being to the rear of the audience form, where a dozen tables with radical books, papers, bumper stickers, etc., were on sale. The mood of this day was more relaxed than at most meetings of this type. The presence of so many family units with baskets of food seemed to provide a casual mood to the affair.

At 3:03 , people who had been sitting to the extreme left of the speakers' platform, began to stand and face away from the common focus to an area not visible from my area located in the center of the audience. Some of them began to move closer to this new focus, other audience members in their vicinity, began to stand and face away from the platform as well.

At this time, there was a moderately loud exhortation from one of the standees to "Come on!" This brought the present speaker to a halt and many more people to their feet. Yet, it was still unclear as to what was going on. I personally felt a nervous anticipation of a protester/police confrontation. I had seen them develop this way before.

By 3:06, the whole left side of the audience had departed or was in the process of following those who had already left. At this point, several leaders on the platform asked the rest of us to "sit tight." They should have saved their breath, as by now, the general excitement and running, and walking flow of people was taking place amid much verbalized but unanswered questions, such as "What was going on?"

When I gained the new area, the cause of all the commotion was clearly visible. From a chartered bus, a group of approximately forty uniformed sailors had descended and were milling about. Shortly thereafter, a petty officer called them to attention. It was a most remarkable sight, and the people began to cheer these men as they proceeded to march towards the speakers' platform. This reaction to what was unfolding in front of us, was not only in appreciation of the symbolic impact, but, also for the fact that their presence was a real act in a real world with unpleasant consequences lying in store for these men. For when military personnel publicly display themselves at antiwar meetings, they thereby ensure themselves of official reprimand

and reprisal. The crowd's applause and cheers went on for two minutes and 15 seconds, with an intensity I have seldom seen before.

In the above situation, people "read" the change in the left side of the audience form, as indicating: (a) a breakdown in audience activity and (b) some new activity emerging. As the left side of the audience form totally lost its shape, the new migratory activity took on a quite distinct form. At this point people from all locations in the audience began to move towards the new focus. With surprising quickness, this migratory form then came to extend as a large swath across the middle of the before solidly packed audience form (see Figure 5.8). Without

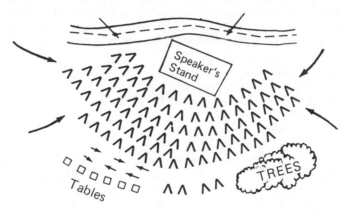

Figure 5.7 Rally assemblage

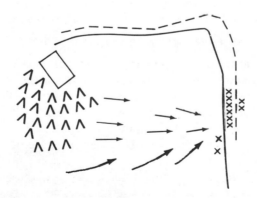

Figure 5.8 Early phase of form alteration

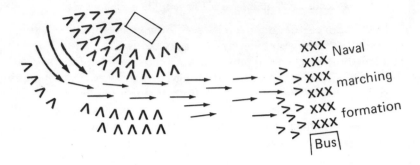

Figure 5.9 Advance form alteration

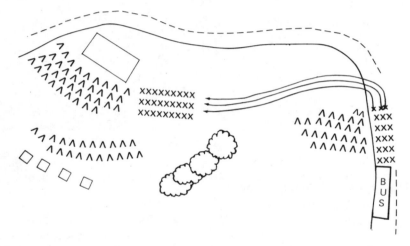

Figure 5.10 Navy personnel march to speaker's stand

knowing any reason or goal, people were seeing, being attracted to, and joining into a new form. The situation became transformed.

A change in a form is not only an occasion calling forth a refocusing; it is a period in which reinterpretation of the situation takes place. Given the sparsity of verbal interactional feedback associated with form reading, any interpretation is subject to more possible error as contrasted with a small group setting. At least in small groups, the possibilities for verbal communication between all the group members exists. In situations where this is not the case, the consequence can be disastrous.

In June, 1967, a police permit was obtained to hold a "sidewalk" demonstration to protest President Johnson's appearance at a banquet. As more and more people (estimated at 15,000 plus) poured into the demonstration area, the density of numbers in and of itself began to force people off the sidewalk into the street: "Later, Police Chief Reddin said he gave the order to disperse the crowd when he looked down from the ninth floor window and saw a bulge in the crowd."[13]

Figure 5.11 Bulge in marching form

This "bulge" was interpreted as indicating a politically motivated-intentional change in activity from the permitted "on the sidewalk — only picketing." This bulge was a change in the form which was read as a law and order defiance activity rather than the unintended consequence of there being too many people for the sidewalk to hold. A command was given to disperse the totally police-encircled and tightly packed demonstration:

> The police asked the impossible. Of course, they failed to get compliance. But they were determined nonetheless. They used motorcycle wedges to force an open space between the crowd and police lines. But as soon as they were opened, the density of the crowd forced those in front back close to the police again.
> Then the police struck. They turned dazzling spotlights into the crowd and waded in swinging. They beat everyone they could reach while the crowd reeled back into tighter compression. Women and children were being pushed down underfoot, screaming.[14]

3. **Categorical and Ambiguous Knowledge and the Principle of Consistency.** Forms seem to, at the minimum, communicate categorial knowledge. While it might not be exactly clear what specific activities a particular form represents, a category of possible activities are derivable. For example, when coming upon people collected about something, as in the "dead man incident," the viewer form communicated a "range" of possible activities taking place. Such activities as the viewing of a lifesaving demonstration, or the aftermath of a fight, or the making of a TV show would be typically consistent ones to find associated with this form in this area.

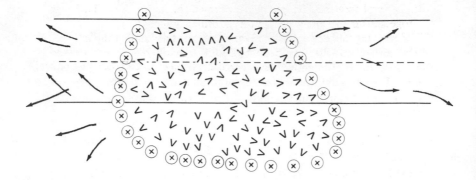

Figure 5.12 Entrapment of crowd by police

Other activities were interpreted as not taking place. This was also accomplished via the use of the principle of consistency. The manifest viewer form is inconsistent with the presence of other possible categories of activities. While I did not know what was going on, I did know that the people themselves were not migrating, fighting, looting, etc. These activities would have produced forms inconsistent with the actual ones present.

The principle of consistency is also at work when one tries to clear up the ambiguity that lies in reading exactly what activity is represented among the possible ones within a category. Note the following account.

DESCRIPTIVE ACCOUNT #15: SUNDAY AT THE PARK[15]

We had been leisurely walking/hiking/exploring our way through the park for about an hour, when the trail led us into a clearing. Having encountered no one in the last twenty minutes, made it all the more surprising to find this area filled. Most people were sitting in face-to-face circles of from four to eight members. Children and teenagers were running about, adding to the festive excitement that seemed to pervade the atmosphere.

My first impression was that we had stumbled into the midst of a counter-culture picnic. Baskets of food, blankets spread out, wine and beer bottles, and long hair were widely in evidence. When a snake line of dancers got started, and more and more people joined in, it became clear that a "Hippy-Happening" was in full swing.

Working our way through the gathering, brought into view an adjacent large field. The open area we were in was just a pocket off this larger one.

The people in the small space could now be seen to be just an overflow of the several thousand people who occupied the larger area. This was altogether far too many people for an ordinary picnic.

Surveying this new tableau, revealed patterns of small group interactions similar to what had been originally encountered. There was no common focus of attention. Everyone just seemed to be having a good time. The basic individual orientation seemed to be small groups facing inward toward one another, engaged in lively conversation. The odor of marijuana filled the air. While there was no common focus, there was a definite density increase in the number of people at the bottom slope of the field as compared to the top. My looking in that direction for a possible focus was interrupted by a blast of a sound so loud, that small birds were literally shaken from surrounding trees. The responding cheer from the people left no doubt as to what was occurring. We had stumbled into the midst of a rock concert that was just getting started.

The first interpretation was that the form reflected a picnic-happening activity. There appeared to be no group focus of attention. Individual elemental spatial relations were repetitively those of people oriented to one another. Other symbols in the setting, e.g., food baskets, were consistent with this interpretation. The discovery of the extraordinary size of the form was a cause for reinterpretation. It seemed improbable that picnic activities could draw so many people to one area. The large size of the total form was inconsistent with the size of the form which picnicking would normally manifest. Finally, the differential density of the location of people within the form became the cue as to the audience nature of the collective activity. The higher density in one area was read as indicating the "down front" of an audience form. The internal structuring of the form was more consistent with this interpretation than the picnicking one.

There is an additional element involved in how forms communicate. This is time and the location of forms sequentially to other forms over the entire career of an event. In the following section, the implications of this are pursued.

4. **Career Location and Knowledge.** The information available to read out of any form can vary according to its location in a series of forms. This is especially true of knowledge that any particular form can communicate about a total event, when it is just one of many forms sequentially appearing in the total event. The overall intention of collective actions, the collective goal, the reason for the assembling of a collectivity, can be read with different degrees of completeness from different forms.

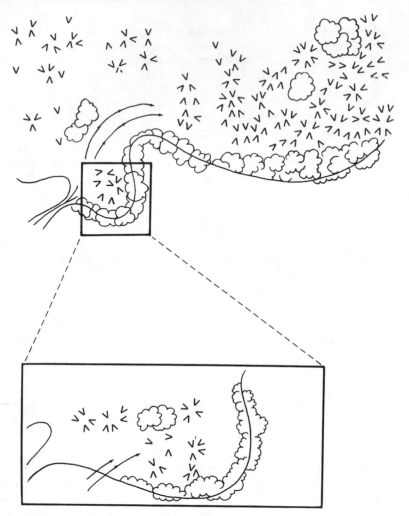

Figure 5.13 Total view of assemblage with inset: first encountered segment of the assembly

Some forms communicate "at a glance" all of the above. A suggestive article by Sudnow[16] can add to our understanding of this. Sudnow has addressed the question "at what point in the course of an individual carrying out an act, can the full act be anticipated or read?" He states that not all moments in a sequence of movements contain the complete order of information as to the nature of the total act of which it is just one part. He goes on to pursue the idea of knowledge of a total act that is available to be read out of a still photograph. In the posed picture situation, the photographer and the subject cooperate in creating a tableau that communicates beyond the moment. The character or disposition of a person is "caught" by this means. In a natural setting, the photographer looks for those moments where a picture "tells a story." Sports photographers are adept at capturing the final moment of a game, e.g., the last basket that communicates the whole struggle that has preceded it.

As discussed in the looting incident, Chapter 2, task accomplishment involves a career of forms. Each of these forms can be considered, in analogy, to any one moment in the movements of an individual carrying out an act. That is different forms emerging out of a sequence of collective actions, have different potentials for communicating the nature of the total event.

The reader is invited to personally test this by watching the evening news on television without the sound. During the course of an average program, such events as demonstrations, picket lines, parades, riots, normal street scenes, etc., might well be shown. What the viewer will normally find is that the cameramen have caught that form which tells the most about what is taking place. Thus, without the sound, the viewer should be able to recognize the nature of the total sequence of events that is available to be read out of the one form presented, e.g., film clippage of a group of looters removing goods from a store, will communicate "looting" as well as the series of forms associated with looting discussed in Chapter 2.

At times, this is not so. A form can be shown that is not clearly understandable nonverbally. During these segments, newsmen often provide verbal accounts or instructions on how to see/interpret what is going on. Narration is used because different forms communicate beyond themselves with different degrees of success.

In television news reporting the technique of verbal overlay can be by-passed by film editing. If the central task form does not communicate, then film footage of adjunctive forms can be added. This provides a career or sequence location of forms leading up to the task form. The effect is to create a visual "narrative" of forms which communicate by virtue of a logic of sequential ordering.

The following excerpt from David Altheide's book *Creating Reality* details how this is accomplished. The careful reader will also see why Altheide subtitles his book, "How T.V. News Distorts

Reality." The sequence that is constructed is not quite a "natural" one.

A cameraman shot this story the following way. First, he got some footage of the crowd moving toward the flagpole. He then filmed them when they arrived, but also included footage of the flag before it was lowered. Next, he framed the flag being lowered, and later, raised again. The key pieces of film were the waving flag and its being lowered. The waving flag was inserted between the film of the crowd moving toward the flag and their arrival. The effect on the television screen was to create a sense of the crowd moving through time by first framing the crowd, then the flag, and then returning to the crowd.[17]

In conclusion, one sees that group forms are a primary feature of collective assemblies. As such, they are used by people as a pragmatic source of information as to what is going on in their situation. Thus nonverbal communication via the reading of forms is a major element in the coordination of collective activities. The understanding of this fact, and the processes by which it occurs, has been the goal of this study.

I would like to close this chapter with some speculative answers to a question generated out of the form-function thesis. If people are continually and routinely "reading" group forms, then why has there not developed an ordinary world-taken-for-granted language that describes group forms? Some tentative reasons for this can be offered here.

First, there is the dominant structural reality of collective assemblies. They exist without communication structures to carry, internally or externally, this type of situationally derived knowledge. And they exist without any institutional or traditional means for assimilating or storing such knowledge. In terms of the broader social structure, there is no permanent group whose interest it has been to develop such knowledge.

Secondly, there is the problem of culturally inherited inappropriate vocabularies. When members of collective assemblies or outsiders attempt to conceptually recreate how they have behaved, they rely on culturally acceptable/legitimate concepts. But these concepts do not necessarily "fit" what actually occurred. Chapter 1 is a small study in the sociology of knowledge. It traces out the scholarly movement away from folk concepts to hopefully more predictive and appropriate vocabularies.

The third factor has to do with the physiology of form perception. Two sociologists, Warren TenHouten and Charles Kaplan, draw upon a large medical and physiological psychology literature to argue that *form perception* is a right brain hemispheric function.[18] The right hemisphere organizes sense data by grasping the whole or geist or the total configuration of relationships in a perceptual field. This is said to produce an intuitive and situationally specific mode of understanding.[19]

Knowing via right brain processes is said to be intuitive, because we frequently find it difficult to reflexively or conceptually objectify this knowledge. This ironic trick of nature seemingly operates such that people can be perceiving, interpreting, and acting in terms of perceptual knowledge without being able to conceptually express how they do it or what that knowledge is.

In discussing the form recognition process of incomplete, fragmented pictures (a Gestalt-completion task), TenHouten and Kaplan state the following:

> The fragments can be seen as a horse and rider and a rabbit only by a simultaneous grasping of all the particular fragments. Recognition does not come about through any sequence of logical operations constituting an analysis of these fragments; words and propositions about the fragments are of no value. Recognition comes about instantaneously; the animals are seen all at once or not at all. The problem is solved not through analysis but through synthesis; such appositional thought consists of silent and non-verbal perception.[20]

We can conclude that the combination of interactional, structural, cultural, and physiological factors that are involved in the reading of group forms is very complex. Our further understanding of the operations of collective behavior will require research that addresses the many questions of levels and types of causal interplay among a large number of factors. Meanwhile people in collective behavior will continue to do what comes naturally. They will create, use, be influenced by, and read group forms as if this book had never been written.

NOTES

1. Sam Wright, Field Notes (July 20, 1974).

2. Robert Sommer, *Personal Space: The Behavioral Basis of Design* (Englewood Cliffs, N.J.: Prentice-Hall, 1969), p. 9.

3. Bronx cheer, boos, screams, jeers, grunts, moans, shrill whistling are all vocalizations that are treated as nonverbal communication. Like explosions, gunshots, crashes, etc., they are not sounds made from combinations of morphemes and phonemes.

4. Ralph H. Turner, "Collective Behavior," in *Handbook of Modern Sociology*, ed. Robert E. L. Faris (Chicago: Rand McNally, Inc., 1964), p. 384.

5. Ralph H. Turner and L. M. Killian, *Collective Behavior* (Englewood Cliffs, N.J.: Prentice-Hall, Inc., 1972), pp. 21-25.

6. Ibid., pp. 30-56.

7. N.E. Miller and J. Dollard, *Social Learning and Imitation* (New Haven, Conn.: Yale University Press, 1941), pp. 232-233.

8. C. J. Couch, "Dimensions of Association in Collective Behavior Episodes," *Sociometry*, 33:4 (1970), pp. 459-460.

9. M. Brown and A. Goldin, *Collective Behavior* (Pacific Palisades, Ca.: Goodyear, 1973), pp. 135-137.

10. For example, see Orren E. Klapp, *Currents of Unrest* (New York: Holt, Rinehart, and Winston, Inc., 1972), pp. 27-28.

11. R. Turner and L. Killian (1972), p. 10.

12. Sam Wright, Field Notes (May 2, 1971).

13. Rodney Stark, *Police Riots* (Belmont, CA.: Wadsworth Publishing Co., 1972), p. 31.

14. Ibid., p. 28.

15. Sam Wright, Field Notes (August, 1972).

16. David Sudnow, "Temporal Parameters of Interpersonal Observation," in *Studies in Social Interaction*, ed. David Sudnow (New York: The Free Press, 1972), pp. 259-279.

17. David L. Altheide, *Creating Reality* (Beverly Hills, Sage Publications, 1976), p. 87.

18. Warren D. TenHouten and Charles D. Kaplan, *Science and Its Mirror Image* (Harper and Row, New York, 1973), pp. 2-30.

19. Ibid., pp. 25-26.

20. Ibid., p. 14.

CHAPTER 6

SUMMARY AND CONCLUSION

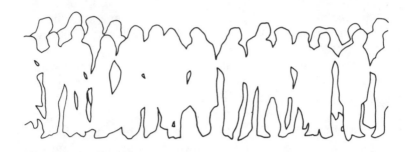

The organization of the collective space created by the bodies of a number of people — **group form** — is one of the few, ever present, *empirically tangible features of collective assemblies.* It exists as a unique "social fact." The group form is not only irreducible to any individual level of explanation, but it has an inescapable and intractable nature. The spatial relations and configurations of people in collective interaction have a "thereness" to them that transcends the symbolic interpretations bounded by any historically specific culture — they cannot be defined away.

These unavoidable spatial manifestations also unavoidably provide historical information about the collective interactions that produce them. Paintings from tenth century B.C., Egypt, from third century A.D., China, and from nineteen century A.D., Eskimos, can each show a procession in movement. The specific cultural meanings and intents of these processions can be unknown to the twentieth-century viewer encountering them in pictures. But the social fact of the group form is there, to be read out of. The culturally transcending message is that a procession is occurring.

Likewise, military leaders in all epics have sought elevated locations adjacent to fields of combat. In this manner, they can keep track of how the battle proceeds. This keeping track is accomplished by the reading out of changes in the spatial forms appearing below. The collapse of the right side of a defense formation instructs the leader as to where to send reinforcements. Again, paintings and carvings from unrelated times and places are interpreted by contemporary observers as battle formations that reveal the presence of group conflict. These scenes are intelligible as battles because we "read" this information out of the presented collective formation. The information on task activities communicated by the forms lives on long after the cultural meanings associated with the cause of the battle activity (task) have been forgotten.

The ability for group forms to communicate across time will continue as long as men gather together in spatial proximity. The common problems engendered in carrying out collective activities produce forms that are similar in all epics despite fundamentally different cultural contexts. This is the basis by which they become recognizable and understandable between symbolic realities.

Any occasion of collective assembly involves two types of activities — task and crowd activities.

1. *Task Activities* — are the activities that members engage in which are particular to the goals, problems of the occasion, e.g., parading, looting.

2. *Crowd (Adjunct) Activities* — the recurring activities which members engage in that are universal to the recurrent goals, problems of being in any situation of collective assembly, e.g., milling, converging.

In the second chapter on task forms, individual elementary spatial relationships were shown to be the building blocks of group forms. The individual's problem of trying to accomplish audience behavior is resolved by the establishing of certain spatial relations and body orientations relative to fellow audience members and to that which is to be the focus of attention. Out of these many individual actions comes an audience form stereotypically identifiable as such.

This form's interdependent relation with the focus, e.g., the paraders, insures a mutual adjustment of individual and collective spatial orientation between the resulting two task forms. The total parade form, an amalgam of the audience-parader forms, can be modified by environmental factors such as constricting streets. But neither culture nor environment can drastically change the individual spatial relation within this form without impeding the practical exigencies that make parade activities possible. Out of practical necessity, the parade form, therefore, comes to transcend any particular occasion of its manifestation.

Chapters 2 and 3 dealt with the career of forms that occur during the implementation of activities. The career discussion prepares us to understand form as a dynamic evolving phenomenon. Both task and crowd forms follow career patterns. In actual collective behavior situations, task and crowd forms are related in a combined sequence that continually repeats itself. It is a career of converging, milling, viewing, task, and diverging which take place around any occasion of collective task activities. This pattern characterizes events of collective assembly. An ancient Roman would not know what a football game is all about. But he would recognize the various phases in the career pattern of the sequence of forms that are involved in the total collective assembly process.

The question guiding this work has been, "How do crowd members create and use forms in nonverbal interaction as a mechanism for coordinating and carrying out collective activities?" The chapters on task and crowd forms examined forms as invariant elements in collective behavior episodes that are, for the most part, creations of nonverbal interaction. The creation of these forms is seen as being fundamentally functional to the coordination and implementation of collective activities regardless of time and place.

The analysis then turned to a consideration of how forms are used in coordinating and implementing collective activities. Both the discussions on group space and forms as media of nonverbal communication, point to uses of forms which are naturally (pragmatically) found in collective assemblies. Again, the implication is that these uses are to be found independent of historical context. The spatial contours emerging about forms serve the primary function of defense. The shape of this contour is negotiated in collective interaction with the direction that the group is facing and its rate of movement being two crucial elements in this negotiation. Other uses of this group space were noted. These include such functions as collective identity maintenance, buffer zones, collective viewing, facilitation, etc.

Group spaces continually affect the interactions between collectivities. Group spaces are also dependent upon and limited in contour possibilities by the forms about which they have emerged. In this manner, forms which are a creation of collective activities, influence the very activities which have produced them: Collective activities manifest forms about which group spaces emerge that affect collective activities.

Finally, the relation between forms and nonverbal communication was explored. The fact that a collective activity will manifest a similar form is a constant that people use in interpreting collective behavior.

From forms, determinations are made about what activities are unfolding, about the amount of support that these activities have, and about what activities one should engage in, and so on.

The interpretations of a form are accomplished by reading out of the particular form what collective activity has produced it. This interpretation process adheres to certain rules, the rules of negative knowledge, changing forms, categorical knowledge and the principle of consistency, and a career sequence logic.

There is a larger point to be made from the observation that group forms have an independence from culture, in terms of understanding how symbolic meanings are made or assigned. For students of situated interactions, there has been a tendency to ignore the fact that meanings are often grounded in and limited by certain material conditions of existence. Symbolic constructions tend to be related only to other symbols. What is real is said to be what people define as real.

But the understanding that spatial permanencies exist in human interaction provides us with an empirical basis for grounding symbolic constructions. Research into the relations of symbols and the material realm at the micro level should benefit our understanding of how meaning imputations are limited and constrained. Given that specific collective activities produce specific forms, then the reading of meaning into these forms is influenced by what is there to be empirically read out of the forms.

The reading of forms is one major area in which future research could be fruitfully directed. Either still or moving pictures of various crowd and task forms could be presented to experimental subjects. Subjects would be asked to identify the form-activity relation in the situation and to elaborate on the cue-reading processes on which these determinations were based.

Out of this should grow listings of forms that are recognizable to most people or to only selective groups, such as police, and these could become the basis for cross-cultural testing. Likewise, the types of configurational cues by which a form is recognized, the rules of interpretation that guide these judgments, and other factors that enter into the total process could be ascertained. The dual goals of this effort would be to make available a more rigorous knowledge of the processes of interaction in collective behavior, and to add to our general theoretical understanding of how human behavior is made meaningful.

APPENDICES

APPENDIX A

METHODOLOGY: PARTICIPANT OBSERVATION
OF CROWDS AND RIOTS

Participant observation is estranging work. One has to be "in" a situation, but removed from it. This requires continual alertness, reflexivity, and alienation. The resultant strain is not to be long endured by any but the most serious student of life.

Participant observation is productively risky work. This method of discovery assumes that either the observer or the situation observed will generate new insights. If this does not occur, then hundreds of hours of time and effort can produce nothing.

Participant observation is systematic work. The gathering of any kind of data requires attention to the dual problems of reliability and validity. Accompanying this are the many practical problems engendered by being a functioning part of that which you are studying. Only through the systemization of procedures can these problems be effectively handled.

The following methodological section details the procedures I used in carrying out my participant observations. The elaboration of how this researcher handled the demands of reflexivity, of systematic data gathering, of concept formation, and of pragmatic survival has more than ordinary importance. Given that methodological guides for doing crowd observations are nonexistent, this appendix hopefully will serve as a resource for future researchers and as a basis for developing more rigorous methods for doing crowd studies.

I. LOCATING CROWDS — BEING IN THE RIGHT PLACE AT THE RIGHT TIME

A difficulty unique to the study of collective behavior is that of being at the right place at the right time. Since a major objective was to study spontaneous or emergent crowd behavior, then a major practical problem was to arrange being present when this occurred. In a sense, there appears to be a contradiction in making plans to be at something that is unplanned. But the fact that emergent crowd behavior is unplanned, does not mean that it cannot be anticipated. This is particularly true of potential confrontation situations and for "expressive crowds."

From 1968 to 1971, the holding of certain types of events carried a high probability of evolving into situations of collective behavior. These were (1) antiwar or Leftist political rallies, protests, parades, etc.; (2) counter-culture rock festivals, happenings, and massive street scenes, etc.; (3) minority demonstrations, protests, parades, etc.; and (4) college campus protests. Some of these events were well scheduled in advance, while others would be literally planned overnight.

In the area in which the study was conducted, this required developing two modus operandi — one for obtaining information about relatively long-planned events and the other for obtaining information about rapidly developing ones. There was great difficulty in simply finding out when an event was scheduled to take place or even that an event was scheduled. In a large metropolitan area, two or three large protests could easily occur without media or widespread public knowledge.

A. LOCAL PLANNED EVENTS.

The local police turned out not to be a good source of information about upcoming events. The police department was organized into geographical divisions. Crowd control is handled at the divisional level. Because there was no central control organization, except for extra large events, there was no central source of information to draw upon. It ultimately proved impossible to establish a contact with each division, who could be relied upon for information. This problem was compounded by the hodge-podge of political communities mixed in and adjacent to the city in which events would frequently take place. Because each of these communities had its own police departments, the metropolitan police had little information about these areas.

The major newspaper and TV and radio stations likewise proved inadequate for my informational needs. Though these organizations gathered data across city boundaries, coverage was lacking in depth. Limitations in the resources that they had available to cover events dictated that they cover only the extra large or significant ones. Unfortunately, knowledge of the large or significant events was as readily available to me as it was to the media. So they offered little to me in terms of information that I didn't already have available.

Attempts to gain information from the groups that scheduled events, were, at first, moderately successful. In 1968, a coordinating committee for antiwar, minority, counter-culture affairs was formed. But, as I was soon to learn, these coordinating organizations were to come and go with regularity. This meant then that in order to get information from the groups themselves, I had to develop contacts with each of the existing organizations as well as the emergent ones. This was an impossible task. Not only were there too many organizations to make contact with, but the ones I did were even more suspicious than the police.

As it turned out, the most thorough, reliable and germane source of information had been at my fingertips from the beginning. This was a local underground newspaper. This weekly publication carried a day-by-day calendar of events for the coming week and month. As an underground paper, the events listed were not the opera schedule, but exactly the Leftist affairs that were prone, at the time, to develop into collective behavior. Despite all my efforts to develop other sources, this newspaper remained the most dependable.

B. RAPIDLY DEVELOPING EVENTS

There are two kinds of rapidly developing events: those which are in response to a significant, well-publicized event, e.g., the bombing of Cambodia; and those which emerge in a situation in response to factors contained within itself.

1. **Externally Stimulated Crowds.** Crowd behavior which comes into being in response to an outside event are the easiest occasions to find out about. Three pieces of knowledge are required: (a) what news a group will find significant; (b) what groups will react to this news as being significant; and (c) where these groups regularly gather for protest or what the significant place is in response to this news.

In most cases regular news reports on important findings, political decisions, etc., were sufficient for making decisions of how political groups would react. In many instances, there had been a build-up in expectations regarding the outcome of an event such as a Congressional vote on a minority issue. The prior build-up usually entailed information as to which groups had tried to do what and where. With this knowledge, what one needed to do was to keep alert for the assembling.

Certain mechanisms facilitate the diffusion of knowledge about rapidly assembling and so emerging events — pamphlets, telephone calls, rumors, excessive police converging on an area, etc. Therefore, I developed a pattern of daily listening to the news, passing through areas where pamphlets were passed out, keeping in regular informal contact with dissidents, and the police. By this means, I managed to keep abreast and attend a large number of these events.

2. **Internally Stimulated Crowds.** Events which emerge in response to something significant within its own setting, were the most difficult to attend — other than by the good fortune of accidentally being in the area. Because these crowds were already assembled, or drew only from their immediate environment, there was no means for me to tap onto the assembling process. Thus, many of those events, which lasted a short duration, were lost to me.

When these events continued long enough for the media to publicize them, then I would converge into their area. There were special difficulties involved in this that resulted in a low payoff in this approach as well: (a) the crowd activities might be over before I got there; (b) the police would have the area cordoned off preventing access to it; (c) large amounts of time would be spent in trying to locate a moving crowd; and (d) in the late 1970's the newspapers and TV in Los Angeles began to play down and even not cover these emergent behaviors unless they went on for many hours.

The rare self-generated emergent events that lasted over half a day were the ones that I could consistently manage to attend. The Isla Vista riots, in the university campus community of Santa Barbara, lasted several days. Despite having to travel 150 miles to an area closed off by the police and at a location with which I was not familiar, I had little difficulty in catching much of this emergent phenomena. Time or duration was the key variable that determined the probability of being able to make observations of totally emergent events.

C. THE CONTINUING EVENT

Overlapping the planned and spontaneous categories are those events which are a part of the continuing career of conflict relations between groups. Some of the events in these relations are planned. Others are situationally emergent. For the continuing events, the cue which I found most important to attend to was the particular stage of the career of the relations. Once groups reached a certain level of disagreement, without their problems being resolved or dominance being established, then emergent behavior could occur at any time.

Under these conditions, I would add on-site visits to my normal procedures. If a minority community was embroiled in a conflict with the police, then I would occasionally visit their area just to familiarize myself with the layout of their area, talk to people for the feeling of who was liable to do what — when, note the location of places where crowd behavior had taken place in the past, and try to be present if something did emerge. It took five weeks of visiting a controversial nude beach before an anticipated crowd incident took place.

D. TRADITIONAL EVENTS

Crowd forms which are traditional, e.g., sporting events, rock concerts, parades, etc., were kept track of with little difficulty. Advertising outlets kept me informed on a regular basis. This allowed a degree of choice in the crowds to be observed. Two approaches were used in this selection. First, a type of event would be chosen for observation, e.g., parades. Second, different kinds of parades would be observed, e.g., Rose Parade, Watts Parade, Fourth-of-July Parade. In this manner, those aspects of forms which distinguish one type from another type were manifested in contrast. Furthermore, variations that are a reflection of just one representative of a form were controlled for.

II. METHODS OF OBSERVATION

A. PREPARATION

1. **Dress.** Since I had decided on a strategy of "passing," much care was given to appearance. Whether working with the police or demonstrators, I dressed as befitting the average for the occasion. This ranged from cutoff levis to sports coat and tie. The success of this was only partial. My Anglo-Saxon physical features make a good percentage of people who see me, on any occasion dressed in any manner, think I'm a policeman. But, despite a couple of very uncomfortable situations, the overall ambiguity created by the dual appearance of the dress versus my physical features seemed to work to my advantage. My legitimacy as a member, or as a nonthreatening observer, was only challenged seriously four times. Each of these was by individuals who I "cooled-out" with whatever story seemed to satisfy them at that particular time.

People tended, in general, to simply leave me alone. I found very few troublemakers or moral entrepreneurs at these events.

There are some rules to clothes wearing that one rapidly learns in observing events which may turn into confrontations: (1) always wear clothes that you can afford to have torn or bloodied; (2) when in doubt as to what is the average attire for the occasion, dress down not up; you are more likely to be correct; (3) always carry at least one large handkerchief or bandana, for its many possible uses, e.g., to wet for tear gas; (4) never wear a ring or a bandana around your neck or any decoration that can get caught on something or by which anyone can grab or twist you. (For women, earrings are particularly dangerous to have on if emergent behavior takes place.); (5) unless it is absolutely incongruous with the setting, always wear shoes (Tennis shoes, or soles with running traction are best. Bare feet or sandaled feet can, and will, be stepped on.); (6) try not to dress so that you look like an undercover policeman trying not to look like an undercover policeman.

2. **Transportation.** I found that by far the best vehicle to use for crowd events was a motorcycle: (1) It solves a problem of parking which always accompanies crowds; (2) If a group breaks up in several wandering bands, it gives one the capability of moving between them; (3) If a police demonstration-confrontation occurs, then simply by being on a cycle, rather than on foot, one tends to be defined and acted toward differently by both conflicting parties, i.e., you are treated as a nonparticipant; (4) It becomes possible to obtain multiple perspectives over an event spread out over a large area, by circling on the motorcycle.

The disadvantages are: (1) one can spend more time riding than note-taking; (2) you are not relating to the world with the same perspective as the nonriders; (3) it is poor to use during bad weather; and (4) a car is more comfortable on long trips or as a shelter to take notes in.

3. **Teamwork.** There are advantages in operating as a team. Goffman makes the point that the presentation of self is seldom accomplished solo.[1] A male-female couple is a natural cover. There is someone to have as company through the many hours and events when "nothing" happens. One also has available a view of the world from another perspective. There are, however, disadvantages. Probably only a dedicated social scientist or a participant could consistently put up with both the tedium and rioting. Therefore, during one or the other of these phases, companions proved to be a hindrance. As a consequence, this approach was dropped early in my observations.

4. **Orienting Observations to Prior Works.** As discussed in the introductory chapter, during the early stages of my research, I was spending a good deal of time going over my sensitizing lists, reading over some of the prior observational notes, and even glancing

randomly through collective behavior textbooks — prior to going out to an event. This slowly changed to where I was essentially just going over prior notes. Even then, only selectively, always asking the same question: "How did I know what was going on here?" This question was then carried into the field setting.

5. **Personal Morale.** I encountered no bigger problem in my research than getting mentally prepared for an event. Overcoming ennui, or overcoming fear or getting in the right frame of mind to where what I was doing would make sense, or overcoming the anxieties of anticipating being "different" in a setting and so challengeable was a constant concern. Creating a sense of value of the effort of the research itself is a problem of concern to all researchers.

6. **Check List.** The last thing that I would do before leaving home would be to go through my check list of items to always take with me. The list was as follows: a new ball point pen, a new notebook, a watch, a jacket (even if going out on a hot day as events often ran into the night), the sensitizing list, my cover letter (this is the letter that I had the department chairman write, explaining my presence at events as being scholastically motivated in case of arrest to hopefully forestall booking), a police courtesy card, sunglasses, pep pills (only used when events went well into the night or for several days), a hat for the sun, and a phone list of my chairman, lawyer, etc.

B. THE APPROACH

Whenever possible, arrival into an area was planned one hour before the scheduled event was to start. This time was used to drive around the whole area, making a map of it — I would note major escape possibilities, cul-de-sacs, likely directions of entrance of police and other groups, and major landmarks for future orientation. This would be followed by a walk through and around the areas that were large enough for collective assembly. This was done to get a feeling for distances, to find and mark high ground that could be used for observation, to familiarize an area to myself in order to at least lessen the fear of the unknown of the physical environment, to get a feel for the normal environment in which a collective behavior would stand as an abnormality, and to be in position when the assembly began.

C. NOTE TAKING

1. **Tapes.** Seemingly, the most practical means of recording one's observations would be a portable tape recorder. Reflections, descrip-

tive accounts, chants, and the general noise milieu could be fed directly into a lapel or a hand-held mike. But, I found that I could not adequately use one and gave it up after two attempts. The difficulties were: (1) I was not used to organizing my thoughts in this verbal manner when for years I had been trained to take notes; (2) I repeated myself without my written notes to refer to; (3) I could not put down a point to come back to, when a lot was occurring and not all could be covered simultaneously recorded at once, and thus, observations were lost; (4) it was difficult to listen to the tape immediately after an event in order to make further comments. This was due to the length of the tape and the difficulties of understanding a great deal of what I had said; (5) one became a prisoner to the machine, which demanded that you attend to it and not the event. One had constantly to be changing the cassettes. The machine was bulky to carry after four or five hours, and it was aggravating to have one's pockets full of tapes and having to worry about protecting the machine when violence occurred; (6) there are far too many instances when people are listening either by circumstance or by design to what the "strange person with the recorder is saying." This, ironically, created not so much an observer effect as an effect upon the observer. Things you want to note are inhibited and, so, therefore, lost.

2. **Written Notes.** For myself, the best strategy for recording observations turned out to be by pen and notebook. Upon first entering an area, I would always make notes of the following for setting the stage. *Who* is holding *what, when,* and *where.* What is the weather — temperature, sun or not, prediction for the day. What is the relational history of this group, or type of event with others? What conflicts are likely to develop? What is the specific cause or occasion of this assembly?

After mapping the area, I would sit, stand, walk, or run with notebook in hand, jotting down my observations. The procedure was to first make an observation, then, to note the exact time in the left-hand column and then to write either an extensive comment or a brief "memory jogger" notation. The extensive note was usually of the direct observation — the idea being to record on the spot what I saw rather than to try to recreate or reconstruct later. The memory joggers were the ideas, or insights, which could be quickly noted, so not to be lost, for development later, under better conditions.

This procedure was not without its problems: (1) One's attention is taken away from the focus while writing. As a consequence, there are times when you take only "memory jogging" notes of the action or lose pieces of it altogether. (2) It is difficult to write while walking or running. This became less and less a problem with practice.

3. **Observer effect.** This classic concern of field work is not the same type of problem in the study of crowds as it is in small group settings. Most discussions of observer effect focus on the uncontrollable influence of the observer on interactional outcomes. That is, how, despite all controls that are exercised, the observer's sheer presence, in a situation with a limited number of people, is still a major "unnatural" factor in that situation.

With the exception of the situations discussed below, this is not usually the case in crowd situations. Though a note-taking person is far from anonymous in a crowd, he is most unlikely to be an effect on the outcome of the interaction. The physical presence of one more body among many is hardly a factor in lending support to or detracting from courses of action. The passivity of the note-taker amongst cameramen, picketers, protesters, chanters, counter-rioters, rock throwers, etc., make him a very minor character in a setting.

This does not mean that note taking goes unnoticed, or unremarked by others. People will look over your shoulder in order to see what you are writing. They will ask you questions as to your intent: "Whatcha doing, writing a book?" In some instances you will be suspected of being a police person and must acount for yourself: "Why are you doing that?" In other cases, you will be more directly challenged; "Are you a cop?" The observer effect on those individuals about you, as distinct from the crowd as a whole, have to be handled carefully to prevent them from becoming an object of collective focus.

This was usually accomplished with the straightforward answer: "I study crowds." Most people would accept this as a legitimate but strange account for one's activities. On some rare, and very uncomfortable occasions, this would not be accepted. The "cop" label would be insisted upon. If discussions failed to change these definitions held by a few others, I found the best procedure to be to move away and try to stay away from those people for the rest of the day.

Therefore, in note taking, in crowd situations, there is always the potential for the "observer effect." This would be true anytime the observer became an object of collective attention. Ordinarily, this possibility could be controlled. There is one important exception. That is when the crowd you wish to study is homogeneous in some externally apparent way in which your own personal characteristics do not match. If a demonstration is small, and everyone knows one another, of if the group is all Chicano or Black, or if a uniform mode of dress is displayed, and you do not fit in, then to mingle with them is to become a common focus, an object of the crowd's collective attention. Once realizing this, I avoided this observer effect simply by not mingling with these types of groups. Given that crowds draw attention, it was seldom a problem to join the onlookers rather than mingling with the actives themselves. From the location of the onlooker, observations could be made without influencing that which was to be observed.

D. OBSERVING

What one wishes to record while observing effects and *how* one goes about observing: though I was not sure what behaviors I would study, I did know from the beginning that, substantively, I wanted to focus on the "situated interactions of large collectives." The following are problems encountered in carrying this out.

1. **From Who's Perspective to Observe.** Whether as active participant or crowd control agent, police are normally present at most collective assemblies. For six months, I cultivated contacts and attended events with police cooperation — usually with an undercover policeman. During this time, I concentrated on obtaining their definitions of the various situations, the kinds of practical problems they become involved with in crowd control, the tactical-strategical procedures of employment of men, the problems of communication, the problems of a field command post, and I ascertained the hierarchies of order giving, and when allowed, attended post event reviews.

Ultimately, I abandoned this relationship for a combination of reasons brought to a head by an ethical question. I began to get a diminishing informational return out of being with the police. Once having been exposed to the procedures, I found the accompanying undercover police to be a burden (as mentioned under the discussion of teamwork). Their need for social interaction during long, boring affairs made it difficult for me to take notes without being rude. In other words, being a social "other" interfered with the studying of the issues before me. High ranking police became overprotective of my welfare. They warned me to withdraw behind their lines in confrontation situations. My refusal to do so led to the next problem. Despite the mutual agreement from the beginning that I was an observer and would not aid in *any* policing activities, I was more and more frequently asked to be a help in — pointing out leaders, transmitting plans of actions of radical groups, giving my opinions of how I thought things were going or were going to go for an event, and providing my estimations of how things went after an event, etc. My refusal made everyone uncomfortable.

Later, during a student demonstration at UCLA, the sociology office was barraged with a series of phone messages asking Sam Wright to contact so and so of the police department. This created such a "nasty" situation between the department Marxists and myself, that I dropped all further dealings with the police. To this very day, several of these Marxists believe me to be a "police fink." There was no problem dropping my contacts with the police or my decision to operate alone. By this time, I realized that the data I was after did not need the definitions of realities of the others in the situations (as explained in the methodology section).

2. **Where to be When Observing.** For events that were located in one area, e.g., a mass picketing action of a building, a routine of movement was developed that involved placing oneself in various perceptual relations with the ongoing activities. First, there was a need to have an overview. Therefore, a series of "high-ground" or elevated locations would be established throughout the area. I would observe from one high location, and then move down into and become involved in the main ongoing activities — e.g., I would complete a couple of picketing circuits. After this, I would move to an intermediate audience position and observe here for a while. Finally, I would end up at one or the other overview positions.

If a group was moving, I would, whenever possible, try to join in. The best location was to be somewhere near the front such that a buffer of bodies existed between oneself and any possible confrontation, but close enough that one could see as interactions developed. When it was impossible to join, paralleling the group movement was adopted as a second-best strategy.

Whenever a mass conflict developed, then a variety of viewing relations would be used. Two elements would determine from where one would view: (a) the best location that allowed one to watch the unfolding interactions; and (b) the position that minimized the dangers inherent in such situations. Since the objective is to observe, more weight is given to gaining a viewing position than is given to gaining a safe one.

E. DANGERS IN OBSERVING

There appear to be many reasons for the lack of serious study of crowd behavior. It is not a respectable study matter. There is little professional or practical real world gains accruing from studying this subject. (Most departments do not even offer courses in collective behavior.) Despite all the riots of the 1960s and the ballyhoo for more research, there has been and still is, little economic support available for the serious student of crowd behavior. It is difficult to study the subject due to its ephemeral nature. The lack of traditional guiding methodology in sociology to aid in this complicates the actual study of crowds. Finally, it has elements of danger attached to it.

These dangers are of two kinds: those stereotypical and mostly nonreal dangers which are shared by most sociologists with the lay person, and those ongoing interactional problems within crowd settings which involve some real physical risk if improper decisions are made or if luck runs against one.

In my futile attempts to obtain funding, I constantly ran into stereotypes of dangers which, in part, were offered as reasons for nonsupport. In February 1969, the UCLA Social Science Grant Advisor best expressed this definition of the situation: "What's there to study? A group of people go mad and the police have to deal with them. You could get killed out there for no reason. Now, who would sponsor this — it's not a proper subject for research and what could possible be gained?"

One of the first dangers the novice observer of crowds encounters is an inability to distinguish between the supposed folk understandings of the dangers and the actual dangers. While types of dangers can be listed, only constant alertness, "common sense" and luck can keep one out of trouble in any particular set of circumstances.

1. **Cul-de-sacs.** The most common of the dangerous situations is to be trapped or cut off from free exit from an area. In police confrontations, this can result in beating and/or an arrest. Always place oneself so that there are a maximum number of exits available. Beware of police tactics of encirclement, running sweeps, and quick changes in directions of movement. Particularly dangerous is a circumstance where tear gas is fired over a crowd's head, landing behind them, cutting off what was before a wide avenue of egress. In this case, lots of luck!

2. **Panic or Flight Behavior.** There are some situations in which a crowd will become densely congregated, e.g., a storming of a building,

the closing off of a building, the rush toward something of attraction (police, a minority, some significant symbol). If caught in the middle under these conditions, it is vital to quickly work one's way to the edge of the crowd. If possible, place oneself at the side rather than the rear of the crowd. Such groups will often engage in about-face flight behavior when resistance or counterattack occurs. To be caught in the middle of this is to know the true meaning of helplessness. The weight of densely-packed bodies all shoving and pushing to move away from a location, produces tons of pressure. At best, one gets out of the situation with bruises, at worst, getting trampled with possible serious injury.

3. **Complimentary Behavior.** In unfolding situations of violence, there are certain role behaviors that one should avoid. These are behaviors that invite others to become engaged towards one's self in a complimentary manner of aggression. While police moving into a situation will strike out at anyone at random, they will focus specifically on those who begin to run directly in front of them. Seemingly, when someone runs like this, there is a complimentary functional vacuum created which draws the police into the role of giving chase, i.e., if you are in a situation where they are going to get you anyway, don't run.

Following the same logic, move out of areas from which rocks, bottles and other missiles are emanating. These behaviors call for an aggressive response which becomes directed at anyone in the area. On the other hand, if the situation is such that one group is attacking another (Blacks vs. Whites, Pro-Jews vs. Anti-Jews), then avoid behavior associated with either one of the active parties.

4. **Emotional Involvement.** Emotional involvement is to be distinguished from emotional contagion. It should be assumed that an observer has enought sociological perspective and maturity not to become totally carried away by an event, so that the analytic role is abandoned. But it is difficult not to become emotionally involved in choosing sides in the situation or reacting to injustices. Though this involvement can be beneficial for understanding others' emotional states, it can also lead to bad decision making. Ultimately, it can lead to injury or arrest.

Consequently certain behaviors should be avoided. Do not go to the aid of someone being beaten by the police. Only go to the aid of someone being beaten by nonpolice, and then only if a possible effect can come of this other than yourself being beaten. Never throw anything at anyone. Only the innocent are hurt and you can be singled out for special counterattack. Unless there is some theoretical rationale, remove oneself from sit-ins, illegal marches, etc., before arrests begin. The point is, never become so emotionally involved that you lose sight of your purpose for being there — to be gathering data, not to save the world or to protect the innocent.

5. **Minority Status.** Never enter a situation where you are a visible minority. "Minority-hood" is a possible symbol around which trouble could develop. Make sure that you are either (1) with several of the major members who would legitimate you, if necessary, (2) with the leadership or with their permission, or (3) with the police. Otherwise, do your observations outside the crowds.

F. OBSERVER EFFECT

There is a danger that is solely associated with being a professional observer. When I first became aware of this in my eleventh month of observing, it was a moment of real fear. This was the realization that by having attended so many different crowd events, I had become visible to certain radical groups and police counterinsurgent organizations. That each from its own perspectives had "plans" for my body to experience. This information came to me in a rapid sequence. At my fifth Chicano protest demonstration, I was sitting on a curb taking notes, when a small car pulled up beside me, stopped, and my picture was taken before the car sped off. It was all I could do to keep calm enough to remain at this particular event and complete my note taking. The car's occupants were Chicanos and I did not know what meaning to give to this picture-taking act. I did know that I became instantly paranoid towards all the Chicanos around me.

During the next week, I spent a lot of time trying to make and keep various appointments with Chicano leaders. To them, I explained my reasons for attending the various events and my present fear. Though none would admit any knowledge of the picture-taking, I was finally referred to someone who said, "It is good thing that you have come to us and I would not worry about it any more."

Two days after this event, I got a call from someone from one of the divisions of the police department. He said that officers from a "nonofficially existent" organization in the department were making inquiries about me. It seems that they, too, had photos taken of me, e.g., at a "homosexual protest, the Watts Parade, a rock concert, and other affairs." They wanted to know, "Who is this guy?" This individual told me that it was fortunate for all concerned that one of the photos showed the two of us talking. It was therefore, possible to legitimize my presence.

Both groups were prepared to cast me into a villainous role and then act according to their imputations. For the serious observer, the following precautions are suggested: If you attend several of a group's affairs, then explain yourself to their leaders. If someone takes your picture, go up and ask them who they are. Even if they do not tell you, explain your status to them. Always have contacts with the police. In general, be sensitive to the build-up in group relations such that these kinds of tactics can be anticipated and so you can avoid being caught in between.

G. TERMINATION

Since the interactions of interest were those of collective assembly, observations did not end when the formally planned, or the organized phase, of the event came to a close. Affairs would be observed until the transition from collective copresence to a "normal" environment was completed. This follow-through is important for two reasons.

1. **Residual Interaction.** It is easy to lose sight of the fact that collective interaction is still occurring after an event has formally come to an end. Clusters of people frequently remain in an area long after the event is over. Those who leave, do so in a collective coordinated effort with other departees. Often, groups will migrate from one area to another, holding mini-rallies and discussion-planning sessions for later affairs. All these collective interactions are direct continuations of the formal occasion. All are still collective interactions.

2. **Instability in the Termination Phase.** This is often the most potentially volative period of a collective interaction. At this time, interactions become organizationally unstructured. Leaders have relinquished control of the assembly. Audiences, picketing, parades, and other types of structured relationships have been terminated. When this happens, people fall back on cultural rules of behavior for the leaving of an area with others.

This situation is conducive for the emergence of new collective actions in response to a symbolic incident or act, a self-declared leader, a disturbance, a collective action of minority, etc. In crowd situations, formal organized controls, once demobilized, are usually impossible to reorganize to deal with emergent situations. In the homosexual protest, the return to the park is an example of how unstable this phase of the collective interactions can be.

Finally, the observer must remain in an area to catch any signs that today's diffusion of people back into a normal environment is only temporary. Many of the major neighborhood riots of the 1960s would stop during the daylight hours to resume during the night. Many of the "commuter college" riots would stop in the evening to resume the next day. It is frequently during the milling of the termination phase, that the discussion will take place about the possibilities for tomorrow.

My own procedures for covering the termination phase generally involved observing the major action arteries of egress. If people in general appeared emotionally riled, or a group appears apparently bent on creating "action," then I would follow on foot or by vehicle. If nothing occurred I would return to the site of the original termination. Here I would join in whatever milling was taking place in that area. When those remaining were reduced to a few in number, I would then get in my car (or on my motorcycle) and do one last broad sweep of the area before heading home.

IV. POST-EVENT TASKS

Timing often demands that two activities be simultaneously carried out following an event. These are to tape record the observations of the day and to tape the radio and TV news of the day, pertaining to the event.

A. TAPING THE OBSERVATIONS

Participant observation as a method is traditionally criticized for its personalized interpretation, as versus the "objective" nature of data gathering. While nothing can be done about the "person" being the recording instrument, steps were taken for control of unintended personal biases, particularly the dangers of the construction of an event from memory.

Therefore, immediately upon the termination of an event, I would proceed immediately to my home, there with my notes before me, I would begin to record the account of the day's activities. There were two kinds of notes taken; those written in complete detail were simply read into the machine.

The other notes were usually just a few phrases or two. These were not repeated into the recorder, per se. Instead, the occurrence, reaction, idea, etc., which these phrases stood for would be elaborated on at this time.

After completing the chronological account of these notes, I would then take the sensitizing list (see Appendix B) and read through it. Ideas, forgotten items, etc., so stimulated would then be recorded. Following this, a list of research ideas, reflections from previous events which I wanted to follow up on, and any questions it had occurred to me to ask about these realities, were read through. Ideas so produced were recorded. Items were deleted or added to this list, as needed.

Even for crowd events of short duration, this procedure could take several hours. After a long exhausting day or night (or both) of observing, it took great discipline and a lot of coffee to finish this step in the process. The one time I put this off until the next day was later regretted. The accounts from the notes were not nearly as detailed as usual. The mental focusing effect of the total emersion into thinking and dealing with a phenomenon for hours on end was lost forever. So were many of the ideas that normally accompanied after event reflections.

B. TAPING THE NEWS

When an incident was important enough for media coverage, the following procedure was used.

If a car was used for transportation, then the two local all-news radio stations were monitored. With tape recorder on the seat next to me, I would alternate between the stations, recording the relevant coverages. These news reports were normally quite short under a minute and a half, and took little effort to obtain. Upon returning to the house, the recorder would be set up by the TV. During the early and late news, as many channels as possible would be recorded. Since nonroutine news was often given first, or lead coverage on all of these channels simultaneously, this procedure was less than efficient. Frequently, only coverage of two channels could be obtained.

Since the focus of my study was the situated activities of crowds, no systematic attempt was made to collect news accounts and interpretations of these events; instead, the random reporting was used for its value in: (1) providing information as to official and others' reactions that would indicate future crowd activities; (2) providing filmed footage of an event which could be briefly observed for more note taking; and (3) providing verbal details of the proceedings from the perspective of others; (4) for good insight as to what the cameramen and editors "saw" in terms of crowd forms — as being forms that communicated what was occurring with little need for verbal explanation.

APPENDIX B

SENSITIZING LIST FOR PARTICIPANT OBSERVATION

(The sensitizing list, as I used it, was continually changing. Modifications were made as new thoughts, questions, and observations were generated. Items were also deleted. The list presented here is one used during the later stage of my field work. It is included here as a guide for others to work with and not as a definite statement.)

The following is meant to be a tentative sensitizing listing for participant observation.

The best procedure for using this would seem to be as follows:

1. Respond to background questions where possible.

2. Read through total listings before observations.

3. Make observations.

4. Tape observations and reflections thereon, with emphasis on induction and empirical generalizations.

5. Read through list again — recall observations made that apply.

* * *

History of Event
SES Profile of Area or People
Ideology of All
Power Relations — between group and society.

Definitional Context of Event — from whose view

1. public definitions
2. own definitions
3. expected outcomes

What is the problem, or is there one — from whose view?
What are the potential problems — from whose view?
What is the Event — from whose view?
What is the function of event — from whose view?

1. identity reinforcement,
2. expressive,
3. power reinforcement and creation,
4. action to a goal,
5. planning,
6. earn or raise money,
7. other?

I. TERRITORY — BOUNDARIES

1. **Physical boundaries:** field, trees, hills, streets, buildings, etc.

   a. *constriction* — density to total area

   b. *funneling* — or expansions in area

   c. *number of exits and entrances* into/out of area

2. **Created boundaries:** barricades, police cars, fires, tear gas, police lines, bystanders, fear.

   a. *Constriction* — density in area increased as natural area is artificially reduced.

   b. *Funneling* — created expansion or funneling via tactical formations, e.g., the V-wedge to expand area and reduce density vs. the U-formation to semi-enclose crowd or total encirclement.

   c. *Number of exits and entrances* — probably reduced but could be increased, e.g., permits to use streets, etc.

II. DEMOGRAPHY

1. **Individual or Aggregate Characteristics** — nonrole

   a. sex
   b. age
   c. race
   d. SES — class
   e. occupation

2. **Density**

   a. size of area and crowd density

   b. gross numbers

   c. location of people — bystanders, acting core, police, etc.

   d. growth and decay — rates or frequencies of both

3. **Migration**

   a. Into and out of crowd: (1) by converging individuals, by groups; (2) by passersby being caught up; (3) by crowd moving and picking up individuals or groups.

   b. Within the crowd: (1) front-to-back and vice versa; (2) around the back or within the front; (3) shifts as crowd moves or changes focus.

   c. Of the crowd — where and why?

III. TYPE OF SITUATED REALITY: CONVENTIONAL TO EMERGENT

Audience — only verbal behavior expected
Acting — verbal and activity behavior expected
Emergent —

Temporal Phases of the Reality	Phases of the Reality
1. Prior to beginning	1. Changes of crowd members or proportions of members
2. Beginning	2. Phases of symbol presentation
3. Middle	3. Phases of mood change
4. Intermissions	4. Relations between symbol shifts and crowd response and mood, including symbols calling for or justifying new and old actions
5. Termination	5. Symbols and symbolic process reflecting the express internal state of the people.
6. After termination	6. Problems — that involve interference with original objective of crowd or subgroups of crowds.
	7. Changes of and in definitions of situation.
	8. Processes of collective decision making.

IV. INTERDEPENDENT ROLES, REALITY PRODUCTION AND MAINTENANCE, AND CROWD CONTROL

A. Interdependent Roles

1. *Overlapping* — role networks and so structured realities brought to situation, e.g., dates, families, and types and limitations of situated roles played.

2. *Situated Roles* — involving not situated role interdependence, e.g., officials, police.

3. *Normal Situated Roles* — created and filled independent of other nonsituated roles — anonymity.

4. *Emergent Situated Roles* — keynoting, etc.

B. **Reality Production**

1. Informal and formal organization

2. Tactics and strategies of presentation of definition of situation

C. **Maintenance and Control** (too much to list)

1. How much police are felt needed by police, and others to maintain reality? Why?

2. Symbolic import of police.

3. Normal and successful tactics and strategies for control.

V. **FOLLOW-UP AND CONSEQUENCES OF EVENT**

A. Public reactions and definitions

B. News accounts

C. Police definitions

D. Relation of expected problems and actual

NECESSARY CONDITIONS FOR COLLECTIVE BEHAVIOR

*I. **ACCORDING TO SMELSER:**

Mobilization for action under hostile belief — attacking someone responsible for a disturbing state of affairs.

A. **Structural Conduciveness:** A setting which is either permissive of hostility or prohibitive of other responses — or both.

1. A figure, class or agency to which responsiblity can be assigned.

2. Absence of communication channels for grievances.

3. Demography or situational variables facilitate possibilities of communication amongst the aggrieved.

B. **Structural Strain:** Impaired social relations are present in precrowd situation.

C. **Generalized Hostile Beliefs: Its creation**

1. *Ambiguity:*
   lack of information
   lack of authoritative leadership
   lack of controlling norms
   lack of faith in controlling values

2. *Anxiety:*
uneasiness about unknown threats undefined threat have enormous power for destruction — source unknown

3. *Labeling:* assignment of responsibility of threat to identified agent

4. *A desire to punish,* remove, damage or restrain the responsible agent.

5. *Omnipotence:* exaggeration of ability of attackers to punish or harm the agents of evil.

D. Precipitating Factors

1. Confirm or justify existing generalized fears or hatreds.

2. Introduce new deprivations.

3. Close-off opportunity for peaceful protest.

4. Symbolize a failure which demands explanation and assignment of responsibility.

5. Precipitate outbursts which may lead to others.

6. Circulate rumors about points 1-5.

E. Mobilization for Action

1. *Leadership:*
   (1) emergent
   (2) deliberate instigator
   (3) formal

2. *Organization:* Degree of previously existing structure, ecological factors, and operations of the agencies of social control

3. *Spread of hostile outbursts:*
   (1) real phase: response to condition
   (2) derived phase: free floating

F. Reaction of Social Control Agencies

1. Crowd communication presented

2. Interaction between leaders and followers prevented

3. No vacillation in use of force

4. Officials do not discuss issue, neutral and maintain law and order.

---

* *The points mentioned are abstracted from: Smelser, N.J.,* Theory of Collective Behavior, *(New York: The Free Press, 1963).*

**II. ACCORDING TO TURNER

A. **Social Conditions** — for lack of social cohesion and integrated group action.

1. Value conflict — inadequacy of normative integration, inconsistency between different norms and values.

2. Frustration — due to experiential conflict with culture and societal organization.

3. Communication inadequacy.

4. Social disorganization — and breakdown of social control.

5. New and unstructured critical situation.

B. **Sources of Strain** — giving rise to utopian beliefs.

1. Conditions are getting worse and frustration increasing: The Golden Age reactionary.

2. Conditions are improving, expectations soar beyond improvements.

3. Contact with exemplary groups who have good conditions or who have successfully used collective behavior.

C. **Utopian Beliefs** — Mobilize needs of collective behavior — a hope for better things to come and belief that they reached via collective action.

1. *Milling:* search for socially sanctioned meaning in unstructured situations with action or mood outcomes.
   (1) convergent behavior
   (2) contagion
   (3) rumor

D. **Necessary Elements for All Crowds**

1. Uncertainty:
   situation is ambiguous or unstructured
   no shared pre-existing expectations
   outcome is uncertain

2. Sense of urgency: feeling that something must be done now

3. Communication of mood, imagery and conception of appropriate action.

4. Normative constraints emerging to back up 1, 2, and 3.

5. Selective individual suggestibility

6. Permissiveness

HYPOTHESIS

TERRITORY-DENSITY

Crowds in wide-open space will gather together in closer density than crowds in more closed space in order to make for more crowd feeling.

TERRITORY-MIGRATION

1. Nondirected crowd will follow routes of least effort
2. Highly directed crowds will follow routes of most efficiency.

EXITS

Any perceived closing of exits will have an effect on a crowd.

** *The points mentioned are abstrated from: Turner, R.H., and Killian, L.M., Collective Behavior, (Englewood Cliffs, N.J.: Prentice Hall, 1957.).*

DENSITY

1. The higher the density, the higher the interaction within a crowd.
2. Different densities permit different physical milling possibilities.
3. The higher the density, the smaller the parameter proportionally to number, thereby reducing physical ability to leave.

MOBILITY

1. Movement into, within, and of the crowd is inversely related to the length of time individuals, groups, or the crowds are at one place.
2. Movers and stayers are two types of crowd participants with movers being those who come, look and leave; while stayers come, look, and stay, i.e., selective convergence.

STAYERS

Those closer to center of crowd tend to stay longer than others as density inhibits free leaving and this location implies more involvement, i.e., interaction between the two.

DIVISION OF LABOR

The more interdependent the role division of labor in a crowd with noncrowd related roles, the less likelihood of collective behavior.

The less informal control existing in a crowd as a function of in-and out-of-crowd role interdependence, the more likelihood of the need of police control.

BIBLIOGRAPHY

Aberle, D. F. "The Prophet Dance and Reactions to White Contact," *Southwestern Journal of Anthropology*, #15 (1959) pp. 74-83.

Abrahams, Joseph and L. W. McCorkle. "Analysis of a Prison Disturbance," *Journal of Abnormal and Social Psychology*, #42 (1947) pp. 330-341.

Ackerman, N. W. and M. Jahoda. *Anti-Semitism and Emotional Disorder: A Psychoanalytic Interpretation*, New York: Harper & Brothers, 1950.

Aiello, John R. and Tyra De Carlo. "The Development of Personal Space: Proxemic Behavior of Children 6 through 16," *Human Ecology*, #2:3 (1974) pp. 177-189.

Alexander, Charles C. *The Ku Klux Klan in the Southwest*, Lexington, Ky.: University of Kentucky Press, 1965.

Allekian, Constance I. "Intrusions of Territory and Personal Space," *Nursing Research*, #22:3 (May-June, 1973).

Allport, Floyd H. *Social Psychology*, Boston: Houghton Mifflin Co., 1924.

Allport, F. H. and M. Lepkin. "Wartime Rumors of Waste and Special Privilege: Why Some People Believe Them," *Journal of Abnormal Psychology*, #40 (1945) pp. 3-36.

Allport, G. and L. Postman. *The Psychology of Rumor*, New York: Holt, 1947.

Altheide, David L. *Creating Reality*, "How T.V. News Distorts Events," Beverly Hills, Ca.: Sage Publications, 1976.

Altheide, David L., and Robert P. Gilmore. "The Credibility of Protest," *American Sociological Review*, #37 (February, 1972) pp. 99-108.

Anderson, Albert T. and Bernice P. Biggs. *A Focus on Rebellion*, San Francisco: Chandler Publishing Company, 1962.

Anderson, Walt. *The Age of Protest*, Pacific Palisades, Ca.: Goodyear Publishing Co., 1969.

Aptheker, Herbert. *American Negro Slave Revolts*, New York: Columbia University Press, 1943, pp. 219-227.

Ardey, Robert. *The Territorial Imparative*, New York: Dell Publishing Co., 1966.

Ardendt, Hannah. *On Violence*, New York: Harcourt, Brace & World, Inc., 1969.

Argyle, Michael. *The Psychology of Interpersonal Behavior*, Baltimore, Maryland: Penguin Books, Inc., 1967.

_____. *Social Interaction*, New York: Aldine Publishing Co., 1969.

Asch, S. E. "Effects of Group Pressure Upon the Modification and Distortion of Judgment," in *Groups, Leadership, and Men*, ed. H. Guetzkow, Pittsburgh: Carnegie Press, 1951, pp. 177-190.

Ash, Roberta. *Social Movements in America*, Chicago: Markham Publishing Co., 1972.

Attica: The Official Report of the New York State Special Commission on Attica, New York: Bantam Books, 1972.

Banfield, Edward C. "Rioting Mainly for Fun and Profit," in *The Metropolitan Enigma*, ed. James O. Wilson, Cambridge: Harvard University Press, 1968, pp. 283-308.

Baker, G. W. and D. W. Chapman. *Man and Society in Disaster*, New York: Basic Book, 1962.

Bargar, B. L. *The Law and Customs of Riot Duty*, Columbus: Published by the author, 1907.

Bartlett R. "Anarchy in Boston," *The American Mercury*, #36 (1935), pp. 456-464.

Barton, Allen H. *Communities in Disaster, A Sociological Analysis of Collective Stress Situations*, Garden City, New York: Anchor Books, Doubleday & Co., 1969.

Bauer, R. A. and D. B. Gleicher. "Word of Mouth of Communication in the Soviet Union," *Public Opinion Quarterly*, #17 (1953), pp. 297-310.

Becker, Howard. "Unrest, Culture Contact, and Release During the Middle Ages and the Renaissance," *Southwestern Social Science Quarterly*, #12 (1931), pp. 143-155.

Beloff, M. *Public Order and Popular Disturbances 1660-1714*, London: Oxford University Press, 1938.

Berk, Richard A. "A Gaming Approach to Crowd Behavior," *American Sociological Review*, #39 (June, 1974), pp. 355-373.

Berk, Richard A. and Howard E. Aldrich. "Patterns of Vandalism During Civil Disorders as an Indicator of Selection of Targets," *American Sociological Review*, #37 (October, 1972), pp. 533-547.

Bernard, L. L. "Crowd" and "Mob," articles in *Encyclopaedia of Social Sciences*, New York: 1931-1935; vol. 4, pp. 612-613; vol. 10, pp. 552-554.

Bienen, Henry. *Violence and Social Change*, Chicago and London: University of Chicago Press, 1968.

Billington, Ray A. *The Protestant Crusade, 1800-1860, A Study of the Origins of American Nativism*, New York: Macmillan, 1938.

Birdwhistell, Ray L. *Kinesics and Context*, Philadelphia: University of Pennsylvania Press, 1970.

Bloombaum, Milton. "The Conditions Underlying Race Riots as Portrayed by Multidimensional Scalogram Analysis: A Reanalysis of Lieberson and Silverman's Data," *American Sociological Review*, 33 (February, 1968), pp. 76-91.

Blumer, Herbert. "Collective Behavior," *New Outline of the Principles of Sociology*, ed. A. M. Lee. New York: Barnes & Noble, Inc., 1951, pp. 165-220.

────── . "Collective Behavior," in *Review of Sociology; Analysis of a Decade*, ed. J. B. Gittler, New York: John Wiley & Sons, 1957, pp. 127-158.

────── . *Human Nature and Collective Behavior*, ed. Tamotsu Shibutani, Englewood Cliffs, N.J.: Prentice-Hall, Inc., 1970.

────── . "Social Attitudes and Non-Symbolic Interaction," *Journal of Educational Sociology*, 9 (1936), pp. 515-523.

────── . "Social Disorganization and Individual Disorganization," in *American Journal of Sociology*, 42 (1936-1937), pp. 871-877.

────── . *Symbolic Interactionism: Perspective and Method*, Englewood Cliffs, N.J. Prentice-Hall, Inc., 1969.

Bramson, Leon. *The Political Context of Sociology*, Princeton, N.J.: Princeton University Press, 1961.

Brearley, H. C. "The Pattern of Violence," in *Culture in the South,* ed. W. T. Couch. Chapel Hill, N.C.: University of North Carolina Press, 1934, pp. 678-692.

Brinton, Crane. *The Anatomy of Revolution,* New York: Random House, 1965.

Brittan, Arthur. *Meanings and Situations.* London and Boston: Routledge and Kegan Paul, 1973.

Broom, L. and P. Selznick. *Sociology,* 5th ed. New York: Harper and Row Publishers, 1973.

Brown, E. "Why Race Riots?," in *Lessons from Detroit.* Public Affairs Pamphlet No. 87, 1944.

Brown, Michael and Amy Goldin. *Collective Behavior: A Review and Reinterpretation of the Literature.* Pacific Palisades, Ca.: Goodyear Publishing Co., 1973.

Brown, Richard M. "Back Country Violence (1760-1785) and Its Significance for South Carolina History," in *Loyalists in the American Revolution: Central Participants or Marginal Victims,* ed. Robert M. Calhoon. New York: Holt, Rinehart, and Winston, forthcoming.

Brown, Roger W. "Mass Phenomena," in *Handbook of Social Psychology,* ed. Gardner Lindzey, vol. II, Reading, Mass.: Addison Wesley, 1954. Chapter 23.

Brownless, Richard S. *Gray Ghosts of the Confederacy: Guerrilla Warfare in the West, 1861-1865.* Baton Rouge, La.: Louisiana State University Press, 1958.

Bucher, R. "Blame and Hostility in Disaster," *American Journal of Sociology,* 62 (1957), pp. 475-476.

Bullock, Paul. *Watts, the Aftermath.* New York: Grove Press, Inc., 1969.

Califano, J. A., Jr. *The Student Revolution: A Global Confrontation.* New York: W. W. Norton & Co., 1970.

Campbell, J. S., J. R. Sahid, and D. P. Stang. *Law and Order Reconsidered.* New York: Bantam Books, 1970.

Canetti, Elias. *Crowds and Power.* New York: Viking Press, 1962.

Cantril, H. *The Psychology of Social Movements.* New York: Wiley, 1941.

_____ . "Public Opinion in Flux." *Annals of American Academy of Political and Social Sciences,* 220 (1942), pp. 136-150.

Cantril, H. and H. Herzog. *Invasion from Mars.* Princeton, N.J.: Princeton University Press, 1940.

Caplin, Gerald. "A Study of Ghetto Rioters," *Scientific American,* 219:12 (August, 1968), pp. 15-21.

Caplow, T. "Rumors in War," *Social Forces,* 25 (1947), pp. 298-302.

Carpenter, C. R. "Territoriality: A Review of Concepts and Problems," in *Behavior and Evolution,* eds. A. Roe and G. Simpson. New Haven: Yale University Press, 1958, pp. 224-250.

Carr, L. J. "Disaster and the Sequence-Pattern Concept of Social Change," *American Journal of Sociology,* 38 (1932), pp. 207-218.

Caughey, J. W. *Their Majesties, the Mob.* Chicago: University of Chicago Press, 1960.

Cavan, Sherri. "Interaction in Home Territories," *Journal of Sociology,* 8 (1968), pp. 38-39.

Chalmers, D. M. *Hooded Americanism: The First Century of the Ku Klux Klan, 1865-1965.* Garden City, New York: Doubleday, 1965.

Chaplin, J. P. *Rumor, Fear and The Madness of Crowds.* New York: Ballantine Books, Inc., 1959.

Chermesh, Ran. *A Strike on a Conservative Campus or Crisis in U.C.L.A.* Research paper for Proseminar in Sociology. Los Angeles: June 15, 1970.

Chicago Commission on Race Relations. *The Negro in Chicago.* Chicago: University of Chicago Press, 1922.

Chicago Study Team, to the National Commission on the Causes and Prevention of Violence. *Rights in Conflict.* New York: Bantam Book, 1968.

Chorus, A. "The Basic Law of Rumor," *Journal of Abnormal and Social Psychology,* 48 (1953), pp. 313-314.

Clark, K. B. "Group Violence: A Preliminary Study of the Attitudinal Pattern of its Acceptance and Rejection: A Study of the 1943 Harlem Riot," *Journal of Social Psychology,* S.P.S.S.I. Bulletin, 19 (1944), pp. 319-337.

Clark, K. B. and J. Barker. "The Zoot Effect in Personality: A Race Riot Participant," *Journal of Abnormal and Social Psychology,* 40 (1945), pp. 145-148.

Cohen, J. and W. Murphy. *Burn Baby, Burn.* New York: Avon Books, 1966.

Cohn, Norman. *The Pursuit of the Millenium.* New York: Harper and Row, 1961.

Coleman, J. W. *The Molly Maguire Riots.* Richmond: Garrett & Massie, 1936.

Commission on Interracial Cooperation. *The Mob Still Rides: A Review of the Lynching Record, 1931-1935.* Atlanta: Commission on Interracial Cooperation, 1935.

Conway, M. *The Crowd in Peace and War.* New York: Longmans, Green & Co., 1915.

Couch, Carl J. "Collective Behavior: An Examination of Some Stereotypes," *Social Problems,* 15 (Winter 1971), pp. 310-322.

_____ . "Dimensions of Association in Collective Behavior Episodes," *Sociometry,* 33:4 (1970), pp. 457-471.

Coxe, J. E. "The New Orleans Mafia Incident," *Louisiana Historical Quarterly,* 20 (1937), pp. 1067-1110.

Cromwell, Jr., F. Paul, and R. L. Lewis, Jr. "Crowds, Mobs, and Riots: A Sociological Analysis," *Police,* (September 16, 1971), pp. 30-32.

Cuber, J. F. "The Measurement and Significance of Institutional Disorganization," *American Journal of Sociology,* 44 (1938-1939), pp. 408-414.

Cutler, J. E. *Lynch-Law.* New York: Longmans, Green & Co., 1905.

Dahlke, H. O. "Race and Minority Riots: A Study in the Typology of Violence," *Social Force,* 30, (1951-1952), pp. 419-425.

The Dancing Mania of the Middle Ages. Babington, B.G., Translator. New York: J. Fitzgerald, 1885.

Daniel, V. A. "Ritual and Stratification in Chicago Negro Churches," *American Sociological Review,* 7 (1942), pp. 352-361.

Danzig, E. R., P. W. Thayer, and L. R. Galanter. *The Effects of a Threatening Rumor on a Disaster-Stricken Community.* Study number 10, Washington: National Academy of Sciences–National Research Council, 1958.

Darvall, F. O. *Popular Disturbances and Public Order in Regency England.* London: Oxford University Press, 1934.

Dawson, C. A. and W. E. Gettys. *An Introduction to Sociology.* New York: Ronald, 1948.

David, Henry. *The History of the Haymarket Affair.* New York: Farrar & Rinehart, 1936.

Davies, R. T. *Four Centuries of Witch-Beliefs.* London: Nethuen, 1947.

Dawley, David. *A Nation of Lords, The Autobiography of the Vice Lords.* Garden City, New York: Anchor Press, Doubleday, Inc., 1973.

DeFleur, Melvin L. and Otto N. Larsen. *The Flow of Information: An Experiment in Mass Communication.* New York: Harper & Bros.,1958.

————. "Mass Communication and the Study of Rumor," *Social Inquiry,* 32 (1962), pp. 51-72.

Department of Labor, Riot Commission. *The Detroit Riot: A Profile of 500 Prisoners.* (March, 1968), p. 28.

Diggory, J. C. "Some Consequences of Proximity to a Disease Threat," *Sociometry,* 19 (1956), pp. 47-53.

Disaster Research Group. *Field Studies of Disaster Behavior: An Inventory.* Study number 14. Washington: National Academy of Sciences-National Research Council, 1961.

Douglass, Joseph H. "The Funeral of Sister President," *Journal of Abnormal and Social Psychology,* 39 (April, 1944), pp. 217-223.

Durkheim, E. *The Division of Labor in Society,* G. Simpson, Translator. Glencoe, Ill: Free Press, 1947.

————. *The Elementary Forms of Religious Life,* J. W. Swain, Translator. New York: Macmillan, 1915.

————. *The Rules of Sociological Method.* The Free Press, New York, 1964.

Eckstein, Harry. "On the Etiology of Internal Wars," *History and Theory,* 4:2 (1964-1965), pp. 133-163.

Erskin, Hazel. "The Pols: Demonstrations and Race Riots," *Public Opinion Quarterly,* 31:4 (Winter, 1967-1968), pp. 655-677.

Esser, Aristide H. *Behavior and Environment.* London and New York: Plenum Press,1971.

Etkin, William. *Social Behavior from Fish to Man.* Chicago: The University of Chicago Press, 1964.

Etzioni, Amitai. *Demonstration Democracy.* Washington, D.C.: Center for Policy Research, 1968, p. 10.

Evans, R. R. (ed.). *Readings in Collective Behavior.* Chicago: Rand, McNally & Co., 1969.

Fact Finding Commission, *Crisis at Columbia.* New York: Random House, 1968.

Fanon, Frantz. *The Wretched of the Earth.* New York: Grove Press, Inc., 1963.

Federal Bureau of Investigation. *Prevention and Control of Mobs and Riots.* Federal Bureau of Investigation, U.S. Department of Justice, 1967, p. 31.

Federal Bureau of Investigation. *Prevention and Control of Mobs and Riots.* Washington, D.C.: U.S. Government Printing Office, 1968, Chapter 7.

Festinger, L., D. Cartwright, K. Barber, R. Fleischl, Jr., J. Gottsdanker, A. Keysen, and G. Leavitte. "A Study of Rumor: Its Origin and Spread," *Human Relations,* 1 (1948), pp. 464-486.

Festinger, L., et al. "Rumor in a Primitive Society," *Journal of Abnormal and Social Psychology,* 53 (1956), pp. 122-132.

Festinger, L., A. Pepitone, and T. Newcombe. "Some Consequences of De-Individuation in a Group," *Journal of Abnormal and Social Psychology,* 47 (1953), pp. 382-389.

Festinger, L., H. W. Riecken, and Stanley Schachter. *When Prophecy Fails.* New York: Harper and Row, 1956.

Fisher, Charles S. "Observing a Crowd: The Structure and Description of Protest Demonstrations," in *Research on Deviance,* ed. J. D. Douglas. New York: Random House, 1972.

Fogelson, R. M. "From Resentment to Confrontation: The Police, the Negroes, and the Outbreak of the Nineteen Sixties Riots," *Political Science Quarterly,* 83:2 (June, 1968), pp. 217-247.

———. *Violence as Protest, A Study of Riots and Ghettos.* Garden City, New York: Doubleday & Co., Inc., 1971.

Fogelson, Robert M. and Robert B. Hill. "Who Riots? A Study of Participation in the 1967 riots," in *Supplemental Studies for the National Advisory Commission on Civil Disorders.* Washington, D.C.: U.S. Government Printing Office, July, 1968, pp. 221-222.

Foote, Nelson and Clyde Hart. "Public Opinion and Collective Behavior," in *Group Relations at the Crossroads,* eds. M. Sherif and M. O. Wilson. New York: Harper Bros., 1952.

Foreman, Paul B. "Panic Theory," *Sociology and Social Research,* 37 (1953), pp. 295-304.

Form, W. H. and C. P. Loomis. "The Persistence and Emergence of Social Cultural Systems in Disasters," *American Sociological Review,* 21 (1956), pp. 180-185.

Form, W. H. and S. Nosow. *Community in Disaster.* New York: Harper, Inc., 1958.

Forrest, Earle R. *Arizona's Dark and Bloody Ground.* Caldwell, Idaho: Caxton Printers, 1936.

Fowler, W. W. *The Roman Festivals of the Period of the Republic.* London: Macmillan & Co., 1899).

Fox, V. *Violence Behind Bars: An Explosive Report on Prison Riots in the United States.* New York: Vantage Press, 1956.

Frederickson, George M. and Christopher Lasch. "Resistance to Slavery," *Civil War History,* 13 (1967).

French, J. R. P. "The Disruption and Cohesion of Groups," *Journal of Abnormal and Social Psychology,* 36 (1941), pp. 361-377.

———. "Organized and Unorganized Groups Under Fear and Frustration," *Authority and Frustration,* University of Iowa's Studies, Studies in Child Welfare, 20, Iowa City: University of Iowa Press, 1944, pp. 231-308.

Freud, Sigmund. *Group Psychology and the Analysis of the Ego.* J. Strachey, Translator. London: Hogarth, 1922.

Fritz, G. E. and H. B. Williams. "The Human Being in Disasters: A Research Perspective," *Annual of American Academy of Political and Social Sciences,* 309 (1957), pp. 41-51.

Fulton, Maurice G. *History of the Lincoln County War.* Ed. Robert N. Mullun. Tucson, Ariz.: University of Arizona Press, 1968.

Gamson, William. *Power and Discontent.* Homewood, Ill.: The Dorsey Press, 1968.

Garfinkel, H. *When Negroes March: The March on Washington Movement in the Organizational Politics for F.E.P.C.* Glencoe, Ill.: The Free Press, 1959.

Genovese, Eugene D. "Rebelliousness and Docility in the Negro Slave: A Critique of the Elkin's Thesis," *Civil War History,* 13 (1967), pp. 293-314.

Glasser, D., N. Polansky, and R. Lippet. "A Laboratory Study of Behavioral Contagion," *Human Relations,* 4 (1951), pp. 115-142.

Glick, C. E. "Collective Behavior in Race Relations," *American Sociological Review*, 13 (1948), pp. 287-294.

Gluckman, M. *Rituals of Rebellion in South-East Africa.* Manchester: Manchester University Press, 1954.

Goffman, Erving. *Behavior in Public Places.* New York: The Free Press of Glencoe, 1963.

———. "The Nature of Deference and Demeanor," *American Anthropologist*, 58 (June, 1956), pp. 473-502.

———. *The Presentation of Self in Everyday Life.* Garden City, New York: Doubleday, Anchor Books, 1959.

———. *Relations in Public.* New York: Harper Colophon Books, 1972.

Gordon, Leonard. *A City in Racial Crisis.* New York: Willim C. Brown & Co., 1971.

Governor's Commission on the Los Angeles Riots. *Violence in the City, an End or a Beginning.* Los Angeles, Ca.: 1965.

Gowen, B. S. "Some Aspects of Pestilences and Other Epicemics," *American Journal of Psychology*, 18 (1907), pp. 1-60.

Graham, Hugh D. and T. R. Gurr. *Violence in America, Historical and Comparative Perspectives.* New York: Bantam Books, Inc., 1969.

Grant, Joanne. *Black Protest, History, Documents, and Analysis: 1619 to the Present.* Greenwich, Conn.: Fawcett Publications, Inc., 1968.

Gray, J. Glenn. *The Warriors, Reflections of Men in Battle.* New York: Harper & Row, Inc., 1959.

Gresham, Hugh C. *The Story of Major David McKee, The Founder of the Anti-Horse Theif Association.* Cheney, Kansas: Hugh C. Gresham, 1937.

Grey, Zane. *To the Last Man.* New York: Harper, 1922.

Grimshaw, Allen D. "Actions of Police and Military in American Race Riots," *Phylon* (Fall, 1963), p. 288.

———. "A Study in Social Violence: Urban Race Riots in the United States," Unpublished Ph.D. dissertation, University of Pennsylvania, 1959.

———. "Factors Contributing to Colour Violence in the United States and Britain," *Race*, 3 (May, 1962).

———. "Lawlessness and Violence in the United States and Their Special Manifestations in Changing Negro-White Relationships," *Journal of Negro History* (Jan. 1957), pp. 52-72.

———. "Police Agencies and the Prevention of Racial Violence," *Journal of Criminal Law, Criminology, and the Police Science*, 54 (March, 1963), pp. 111-113.

———. *Racial Violence in the United States.* New York: Aldine Publishing Co., 1969.

———. "Three Major Cases of Colour Violence in the United States," *Race*, 5 (July, 1963), pp. 76-86.

———. "Urban Racial Violence in the United States Changing Ecological Considerations," *American Journal of Sociology*, 66 (September, 1960), pp. 102-119.

Grosser, D., N. Polansky, and R. Lippitt. "A Laboratory Study of Behavioral Contagion," *Human Relations*, 4 (1951), pp. 115-142.

Gruenberg, E. M. "Socially Shared Psychopathology," in *Explorations in Social Psychiatry*, A. H. Leighton. New York: Basic Books, Inc., 1957).

Guevara, E. Che. *Episodes of the Revolutionary War.* New York: International Publishers, 1968.

Gurr, Ted, with Rittenbuerg, Charles. *The Conditions of Civil Violence: First Tests of a Causal Model,* (Center of International Studies, Princeton University, Research Monograph No. 28, Princeton, N.J.: 1967).

Gusfield, J.R. *Protest, Reform, and Revolt.* New York: John Wiley & Sons, Inc., 1970).

———— . *Symbolic Crusade, Status Politics and the American Temperance Movement.* Urbana and London: University of Illinois Press, 1963.

Guthrie, C. L. *Riots in Seventh Century Mexico City: A Study in Social History with Special Emphasis upon the Lower Classes.* Ph.D. dissertation, University of California, Berkeley, 1937.

Hall, Edward T. *The Hidden Dimension.* Garden City, New York: Doubleday & Co., Inc., 1966.

———— . *The Silent Language.* N.Y., N.Y.: Fawcett Publications, Inc., 1959.

Hare, A. Paul. "Non-Violent Action From a Social-Psychological Perspective," *Sociological Inquiry, Journal of the National Sociology Honor Society,* 38:1 (Winter, 1968).

Harris, Meriel D. "Two Famous Kentucky Feuds and Their Causes," Unpublished M.A. thesis, University of Kentucky, 1940.

Hartung, F. E. and M. A. Floch. "A Socio-psychological Analysis of Prison Riots: An Hypothesis," *Journal of Criminal Law, Criminology, and Police Science,* 47 (1956-1957), pp. 51-57.

Hayden, Tom. *Rebellion in Newark, Official Violence and Ghetto Response.* New York: Random House, 1967.

Heaps, W. A. *Riots U.S.A., 1765-1965.* New York: Seabury Press, 1966.

Heaton, J. W. "Mob Violence in the Late Roman Republic," *Illinois University Studies in the Social Sciences,* 23 (1938-1939), Urbana, Ill.: University of Illinois Press, 1939).

Heberle, Rudolf. *Social Movements: An Introduction to Political Sociology.* New York: Appleton-Century-Crofts, Inc., 1951.

Hecker, J. F. K. *The Black Death in the Fourteenth Century.* Babington, B.G., Translator. London: A. Schloss, 1833.

Hediger, H. *Studies of the Psychology and Behavior of Captive Animals in Zoos and Circuses.* London: Butterworth Scientific Publications, 1955, pp. 40-42.

Hersh, Seymour M. *My Lai 4, A Report on the Massacre and Its Aftermath.* New York: Random House, 1970).

Hershey, John. *The Algiers Motel Incident.* New York: Alfred A. Knopff, Inc., 1968.

Hibbert, C. *King Mob: The Story of Lord George Gordon and the London Riots of 1780.* Cleveland: The World Publishing Company, 1958.

Hiller, E. T. *The Strike: A Study in Collective Action.* Chicago: University of Chicago Press, 1928.

Hobsbawm, E. J. "Economic Fluctuations and Some Social Movement since 1800," *Economic History Review,* 2nd Series, 1 (1952), pp. 1-25.

———— . "The Machine Breakers," *Past and Present,* (Feb. 1952), pp. 57-70.

———— . *Primitive Rebels: Studies in Archaic Forms of Social Movement in the 19th and 20th Centuries.* New York: W. W. Norton and Sons, Inc., 1959.

Hoffer, E. *The True Believer.* New York: New American Library, 1958.

Hofstadter, Richard. *The Progressive Movement 1900-1915.* Englewood Cliffs, N.J.: Prentice-Hall, Inc., 1963.

Hofstadter, Richard and Michael Wallace. *American Violence.* New York: Random House, Inc., 1971.

Horn, S. F. *Invisible Empire: The Story of the Ku Klux Klan, 1866-1871.* Boston, Mass.: Houghton Mifflin, 1939.

Horowitz, I. L. "The Struggle is the Message: Tactics, Trends, and Tensions in the Anti-War Movement," Position paper prepared for the National Commission on the Causes and Prevention of Violence. Third draft: Sept. 23, 1968, mimeograph.

Hovland, C. I. and R. R. Sears. "Minor Studies in Aggression: VI, Correlations of Lynchings with Economic Indices," *Journal of Psychology,* 9 (1949), pp. 301-310.

Howard, J. R. *The Cutting Edge.* Philadelphia, New York: J.B. Lippicott Co., 1974.

Hudson, Bradford B. "Anxiety in Response to the Unfamiliar," *Journal of Social Issues,* 10 (1954), pp. 53-60.

Hull, Clark L. *Hypnosis and Suggestibility.* New York: Appleton-Century-Crofts, Inc., 1933.

Hurry, J. B. *Vicious Circles in Sociology and Their Treetment.* London: J. & A. Churchill, 1915.

Hurwitz, Ken. *Marching Nowhere.* New York: W. W. Norton, & Co., 1971.

Jackson, M., E. Peterson, J. Bull, S. Monsen, and P. Richmond. "The Failure of and Incipient Social Movement," *Pacific Sociological Review,* 3 (1960), pp. 35-40.

Jacobs, Herbert A. "To Count a Crowd," *Columbia Journalism Review,* 6 (Spring, 1967), pp. 37-40.

Jacobson, D. J. *The Affairs of Dame Rumor.* New York: Rinehart, 1948.

Janowitz, Morris. *Social Control of Escalated Riots.* Chicago: University of Chicago Center for Policy Study, 1968, p. 7.

Jastrow, J. "Conversion, Religious," *Encyclopaedia of the Social Sciences,* 4 (New York: Macmillan, 1935), pp. 353-355.

Jefferies, Vincent, Ralph H. Turner, Richard T. Morris. "The Public Perception of the Watts Riot as Social Protest," *American Sociological Review,* 36 (June, 1971), pp. 443-451.

Jennings, Humphrey, et al. *May the Twelfth: Mass-Observation Day Surveys, 1937.* London: Faber and Faber: Ltd., 1937.

Johnson, Donald. "The Phantom Anesthesist of Mattoon," *Journal of Abnormal and Social Psychology,* 40 (1945), pp. 176-186.

Jones, Virgil C. *The Hatfields and the McCoys.* Chapel Hill, N.C.: University of North Carolina Press, 1948.

Jorden, Joe. "Lynchers Don't Like Lead," *Atlantic Monthly,* 177 (February, 1946), pp. 103-108.

Jovell, M. *The Chatist Movement.* London: 1918.

Katona, G. *Psychological Analysis of Economic Behavior.* New York: McGraw-Hill, 1951.

Katz, D. "The Psychology of the Crowd," in *Fields of Psychology.* ed. J. P. Guilford. New York: D. Van Nostrand Company, 1940, pp. 145-162.

Keiser, R. Lincoln. *The Vice Lords, Warriors of the Streets.* New York: Holt, Rinehart and Winston, Inc., 1969.

Kelley, Harold H., John C. Condry, Jr., Arnold E. Dahlke, and Arther H. Hill.

"Collective Behavior in a Simulated Panic Situation," *Journal of Experimental Social Psychology,* 1 (1965), pp. 20-54.

Kerckhoff, Alan C. and Kurt W. Back. *The June Bug: A Study of Hysterical Contagion.* New York: Appleton-Century-Croft, 1968.

Kerouac, Jack. *Lonesome Traveler.* New York: Grove Press, Inc., 1960.

Killian, L. M. "The Significance of Multiple-group Membership in a Disaster," *American Journal of Sociology,* 57 (1952), pp. 308-314.

King, C. Wendell. *Social Movements in the United States.* New York: Random House, 1956.

Kinzer, Donald L. *An Episode in Anti-Catholicism: The American Protective Association.* Seattle, Washington: University of Washington Press, 1964.

Kitson, Clark G. "Hunger and Politics in 1842," *Journal of Modern History,* 25 (1953), pp. 355-374.

Klapp, Orrin E. *Currents of Unrest: An Introduction to Collective Behavior.* New York: Holt, Rinehart, & Winston, Inc., 1972.

————. *Symbolic Leaders.* New York: Funk & Wagnall, Inc., 1964.

Knapp, R. H. "A Psychology of Rumor," *Public Opinion Quarterly,* 8 (1944), pp. 22-37.

Knowles, K. G. "Strike-Proneness and Its Determinants," *American Sociological Review,* 60 (1954), pp. 213-229.

Komisaruk, Richard and Carol Pearson. "Children of the Detroit Riots," *Journal of Urban Law,* 45 (Spring and Summer, 1968), pp. 599-626.

Knopf, Terry Ann. "Rumors, Race and Riots," *Social Policy Series* (April, 1974).

Kriesberg, M. "Cross Pressures and Attitued: A Study of the Influence of Conflicting Propaganda on Opinions Regarding American and Soviet Relations," *Public Opinion Quarterly,* 13 (1949), pp. 5-16.

Lader, Lawrence. "New York's Bloodiest Week," *American Heritage,* (June, 1959), pp. 44-49;95-98.

Lammers, Cornelis J. "Strikes and Mutinies," *Administrative Science Quarterly,* 14 (April, 1969), pp. 558-572.

Lang, Kurt and Gladys Engles. "Collective Behavior," *International Encyclopaedia of the Social Sciences,* 2, New York: Macmillan, 1968, pp. 556-565.

————. *Collective Dynamics.* New York: Thomas Y. Crowell, Inc., 1961.

Lanternari, Vittorio. *The Religions of the Oppressed: A Study of Modern Messianic Cults.* New York: New American Library, 1963.

LaPiere, R. T. *Collective Behavior.* New York: McGraw-Hill Book, Co., 1938.

Larson, O. N. and R. J. Hill. "Social Structure and Interpersonal Communications," *American Journal of Sociology,* 63 (1958), pp. 497-505.

Lasswell, H. D. "Agitation," *Encyclopaedia of the Social Sciences,* 1, New York: Macmillan, 1935, pp. 487-488.

Lasswell, Harold D. and Abraham Kaplan. *Power and Society.* New Haven: Yale University Press, 1950.

Le Bon, Gustave. *The Crowd: A Study of the Popular Mind.* London: Ernest Benn, Ltd., 1896.

————. *The Psychology of Revolution.* New York: Holt, Rinehart, Inc., 1913.

Lee, A. M. and N. D. Humphrey. *Race Riot.* New York: The Dryden Press, 1943.

Leighton, A. H. *The Governing of Men.* Princeton: Princeton University Press, 1945.

Leinwand, Gerald and Anita Monte. *Riots.* New York: Washington Square Press, 1970.

Lemberg Center for the Study of Violence. *Riot Data Review*. 3 (Feb. 1969), pp. 1-38.

Lewis, Jerry M. "Review Essay: The Telling of Kent State Social Problems," pp. 267-279.

Lidz, Victor. "A Note on: 'Non-Violence is Two'," *Journal of the National Sociology Honor Society, Sociological Inquiry*, 38:1 (Winter, 1968).

Lipset, Seymour M. *Rebellion in the University*. Boston: Little, Brown and Co., 1971.

Lodhi, Abdul Qaiyum and Charles Tilly. "Urbanization, Crime, and Collective Violence in 19th Century France," *American Journal of Sociology*, 79:2 (1964), pp. 296-318.

Lofland, John. *Doomsday Cult, A Study of Conversion, Proselytization and Maintenance of Faith*. Englewood Cliffs, N.J.: Prentice-Hall, Inc., 1966.

Lofland, Lyn H. *A World of Strange*. New York: Basic Books, Inc., 1973.

Lohman, J. D. *The Police and Minority Groups*. Chicago: Chicago Park District, 1947.

Longly, R. S. "Mob Activities in Revolutionary Massachusetts," *New England Quarterly*, 6 (1933), pp. 98-130.

McCague, James. *The Second Rebellion: The Story of the New York City Draft Riots of 1863*. New York: Dial, 1968.

McCrady, Edward Be. *The History of South Carolina in the Revolution: 1780-1783*. New York: Macmillan, 1902.

McDougall, W. *The Group Mind*. New York: G. P. Putnam and Sons, 1920.

———. *Introduction to Social Psychology*. London: Methuen, & Co., 1908.

McGraw, P. and W. McGraw. *Assignment: Prison Riots*. New York: Henry Holt, 1954.

McLuhan, M. *Understanding Media*. New York: Signet Books, 1964.

McNeill, Don. *Moving Through Here*. New York: Lancer Books, Inc., 1970.

McPhail, Clark. "The Assembling Process: A Theoretical and Empirical Examination," *American Sociological Review*, 38 (December, 1971), pp. 721-735.

———. "Civil Disorder Participation: A Critical Examination of Recent Research," *American Sociological Review*, 36 (December, 1970), pp. 1058-1073.

———. "Some Theoretical and Methodological Strategies for the Study of Crowd Phenomena," Unpublished manuscript. University of Illinois-Urbana, January 1972, p. 7.

———. "Theoretical and Methodological Strategies for the Study of Individual and Collective Behavior Sequences," Paper presented at the annual meeting of the American Sociological Association, August 29, 1972.

MacCurdy, J. T. *The Structure of Morale*. New York: Macmillan & Co., 1943.

MacIver, Robert M. and Charles H. Page. *Society: A Textbook of Sociology*. New York: Rinehart & Co., Inc., 1937.

Mackey, Charles. *Extraordinary Popular Delusions and the Madness of Crowds*. Boston: L. C. Page & Co., 1932.

Madge, Charles and Tom Harrison. *Britain by Mass-Observation*. Harmondsworth, England: Penguin Books, Ltd., 1939.

Maier, Pauline. "Popular Uprisings and Civil Authority in Eighteenth-Century America," *William and Mary Quarterly, 3rd Series*, forthcoming.

Mailer, Norman. *The Armies of the Night*. New York: The New American Library, Inc., 1968.

Mannheim, Karl. *Man and Society in an Age of Reconstruction.* New York: Harcourt, Brace, & Co., 1951.

Mather, F. C. *Public Order in the Age of the Chartists.* Manchester, 1959.

Martin, E. D. *The Behavior of Crowds: A Psychological Study.* New York: Harper & Bros., 1920.

————. "Some Mechanisms which Distinguish the Crowd from Other Forms of Social Behavior," *Journal of Abnormal and Social Psychology,* 18 (1923), pp. 187-203.

Martin, E. W. *The History of the Great Riots.* Philadelphia: National Publishing Co., 1877.

Masotti, Louis H. and Don R. Bowen. *Riots and Rebellion, Civil Violence in the Urban Community.* Beverly Hills, Ca.: Sage Publications, Inc., 1968.

Mattick, Hans W. "Form and Content of Recent Riots," *Midway,* 9:1 (Summer, 1968), pp. 18-19.

Marx, Gary T. *Protest and Prejudice, A Study of Belief in the Black Community.* New York: Harper & Row, Inc., 1969.

Marx, Karl. *The Eighteenth Brumaire of Louis Bonaparte.* New York: International Publishers, 1963.

Meadows, P. "Movements of Social Withdrawal," *Sociology and Social Research,* 29 (1944-1945), pp. 46-50.

Meerloo, A. M. *Delusion and Mass-delusion.* New York: Nervous and Mental Disease Monographs, 1949.

————. *Patterns of Panic.* New York: International Universities Press, 1950.

Medalia, N. Z. "Who Cries Wolf?" *Sociological Problems,* 7 (1959-1960), pp. 233-240.

Mehrabian, Albert. *Non-Verbal Communication.* Chicago: Aldine, Atherton Inc., 1972.

Megargee, Edwin I. and J. E. Hokanson. *The Dynamics of Aggression.* New York: Harper & Row, 1970.

Meirt, N. C., G. H. Mennenga, and H. J. Stolz. "An Experimental Approach to the Study of Mob Behavior" *The Journal of Abnormal and Social Psychology,* 36 (July, 1941), pp. 506-524.

Milgram, Stanley and Hans Toch. "Collective Behavior in Crowds and Social Movements," in *Handbook of Social Psychology,* eds. Lindzey, G. and Aaronson, E., Reading, Mass.: Addison Welsey, 1969, vol. 4, pp. 507-610.

Miller, N. E. and J. Dollard. *Social Learning and Imitation.* New Haven, Conn.: Yale University Press, 1941.

Mintz, A. "A Re-examination of Correlations between Lynchings and Economic Indices," *Journal of Abnormal and Social Psychology,* 41 (1946), pp. 154-160.

————. "Non-adaptive Group Behavior," *Journal of Abnormal and Social Psychology,* 46 (1951), pp. 150-159.

Mitchell, J. Paul. *Race Riots in Black and White.* Englewood Cliffs, N.J.: Prentice-Hall, Inc., 1970.

Morgan, William R. and Terry N. Clark. "The Causes of Racial Disorders: A Grievance Level Explanation," *American Sociological Review,* 38 (October, 1973), pp. 611-624.

Morris, Desmond. *The Naked Ape.* New York: Dell Publishing Co., 1967.

Mullin, Gerald W. *Flight and Rebellion, Slave Resistance in Eighteenth Century Virginia.* New York: Oxford University Press, 1972.

Murdock, G. "The Common Denominator of Culture," in *Perspectives in Human Evolution,* eds. Washburn, S. and Jay P., New York: Holt, Rinehart, & Winston, Inc., 1968.

Murray, R. K. *Red Scare: A Study in National Hysteria: 1919-1920.* Minneapolis: University of Minnesota Press, 1955.

Nelson, Jack and Jack Bass. *the Orangeburg Massacre.* New York: Ballantine Books, 1970.

Nicolosi, A. S. "The Rise and Fall of the New Jersey Vigilante Societies," *New Jersey History,* 86 (1968), pp. 29-32.

Norton, W. J. "The Detroit Riots and After," *Survey Graphic,* 32 (August, 1943), pp. 317-318.

Ortega y Gasset, Jose. *The Revolt of the Masses.* New York: W. W. Norton, & Co., Inc., 1932.

Paige, Jeffery M. "Political Orientation and Riot Participation," *American Sociological Review,* 36, (1971), pp. 810-820.

Park, Robert E. "Collective Behavior," *Encyclopaedia of the Social Sciences,* 2, New York: Macmillan, 1935.

———. "Human Nature and Collective Behavior," *American Journal of Sociology,* 32 (March, 1927), pp. 733-741.

———. *Society: Collective Behavior, News and Opinion, Sociology and Modern Society.* Glencoe, Ill.: The Free Press, 1955.

Park, R. E. and E. Q. Burgess. *Introduction to the Science of Sociology.* Chicago: University of Chicago Press, 1921.

Penrose, L. S. *On the Objective Study of Crowd Behavior.* London: H. K. Lewis & Co., 1952.

Peterson, Richard A. "The Unusual History of Rock Festivals: An Instance of Media Facilitation," *Journal of Music and Society,* 2:2 (Winter, 1973), pp. 1-27.

Peterson, W. A. and N. P. Gist. "Rumor and Public Opinion," *American Journal of Sociology,* 57 (1951), pp. 159-167.

Piaget, Jean. *The Child's Conception of Time.* New York: Ballentine Books, 1971.

Platt, Anthony E. *The Politics of Riot Commissions, 1917-1970.* New York: Collier Books, 1971.

Polansky, N., R. Lippitt, and F. Redl. "An Investigation of Behavioral Contagion in Groups," *Human Relations,* 3 (1950), pp. 319-348.

Porambo, Ron. *No Cause of Indictment: An Autopsy of Newark.* New York: Holt, Rinehart, and Winston, 1971.

Posthumus, N. W. "The Tulip Mania in Holland in the Years 1636 and 1637," *Journal of Economic and Business History,* 1 (1929), pp. 434-466.

Potter, Robert A. and J. J. Sullivan. *The Campus by the Sea Where the Bank Burned Down.* Santa Barbara, Ca.: Faculty and Clergy Observers Program, 1970.

Prasad, J. "The Psychology of Rumour: A Study Relating to the Great Indian Earthquake of 1934," *British Journal of Psychology,* 26 (1935), pp. 1-15.

Prosser, William. "Trespassing Children," *California Law Review* (August, 1959), p. 427.

Proudfoot, Merrill. *Diary of a Sit-In.* New Haven, Conn.: College and University Press, 1962.

Pruden, D. "A Sociological Study of a Texas Lynching," *Studies in Sociology,* 1 (1936), pp. 3-9.

Putney, S. W. and M. L. Cadwallader. "An Experiment in Crisis Interaction," *Resident Study.* State College, Washington, 22 (1954), pp. 94-102.

Quarantelli, E. L. "A Study of Panic: Its Nature, Types and Conditions," *National Opinion Research Center Survey,* (1953), p. 308.

_____. "The Nature and Conditions of Panic," *American Journal of Sociology,* 60 (1954) pp. 267-275.

_____. "The Structural Problem of a Sociological Specialty: Collective Behavior's Lack of a Critical Mass," *American Sociologist,* 9 (May, 1974), pp. 59-68.

Raper, A. F. *The Tragedy of Lynching.* Chapel Hill, N.C., University of North Carolina Press, 1933.

Rawitscher, Audrey. Editor. *Riots in the City, An Addendum to the McCone Commission Report.* Los Angeles: National Association of Social Workers, 1967.

Redl, F. "The Psychology of Gang Formation and the Treatment of Juvenile Delinquents," *Psychoanalytic Studies of Children,* 1 (1945), pp. 367-377.

Report of the President's Commission on Campus Unrest. New York: Hearst Corp., 1970.

Report of the President's Commission on Campus Unrest. William W. Scranton, Chairman. New York: Avon Publishing Co., 1971.

Rich, B. M. *The Presidents and Civil Disorder.* Washington, D.C.: The Brookings Institute, 1941.

Rose, A. M. "Rumor in the Stock Market," *Public Opinion Quarterly,* 15 (1951), pp. 461-486.

Rose, R. B. "Eighteenth-Century Price Riots and Public Policy in England," *International Review of Social History,* 6 (1961), Pt. 2, pp. 277-292.

_____. "Eighteenth-Century Price Riots, The French Revolution and the Jacobian Maximum," *International Review of Social History,* 3 (1959), pp. 432-445.

_____. "The French Revolution and the Grain Supply," *Bulletin of the John Rylands Library,* 49:i (September, 1956), pp. 171-187.

_____. "The Priestly Riots of 1791," *Past and Present,* (Nov. 1960), pp. 68-88.

Rose, Thomas. *Violence in America.* New York: Random House, 1969.

Ross, E. A. *Foundations of Sociology.* 2nd ed., New York: The Macmillan Co., 1905.

_____. *Principles of Sociology.* New York: The Century Co., 1920.

_____. *Social Psychology.* New York: Macmillan & Co., 1908.

Rossi, Peter. *Ghetto Revolts.* New Brunswick, N.J.: Transaction Books, 1973.

Rude, George. *The Crowd in History — 1730-1848.* New York: John Wiley & Sons, Inc., 1964.

_____. *The Crowd in the French Revolution.* Oxford, London: Oxford University Press, 1959.

_____. "The Gordon Riots: A Study of the Rioters and Their Victims," *Transactions of the Royal Historical Society, 5th Series,* 6 (1956), pp. 93-114.

_____. "The London 'Mob' of the Eighteenth Century," *The Historical Journal,* 2:i (1959), pp. 1-18.

_____. "Mother Gin and the London Riots of 1736," *The Guildhall Miscellany,* 10 (September, 1959).

_____. "The Study of Popular Disturbances in the 'Pre-Industrial' Age," *Historical Studies,* (May, 1963), pp. 457-469.

Rudolph, Lloyd I. "The Eighteenth Century Mob in America and Europe," *American Quarterly,* 2 (1959).

Sacks, Harvey. "Methods in Use for the Production of Social Order: A Method of Warrantably Informing Moral Character," *Center for the Study of Law and Society,* University of California, Berkeley, 1962.

Schachter, S. and H. Burdick. "A Field Experiment on Rumor Transmission and Distortion," *Journal of Abnormal and Social Psychology,* 50 (1955), pp. 363-371.

Schapiro, J. Salwyn. *Movements of Social Dissent in Modern Europe.* Princeton, N.J.: D. Van Nostrand Co., Inc., 1962.

Scheflen, M. and E. Albert. *Body Language and the Social Order.* Englewood Cliffs, N.J.: Prentice-Hall, Inc., 1972.

Schuler, E. A. and V. Parenton. "A Recent Epidemic of Hysteria in a Louisiana High School," *Journal of Social Psychology,* 17 (1943), pp. 221-235.

Schultz, Duane P. *Panic Behavior.* New York: Random House, 1964.

Sears, David O. and John B. McConahan. *Los Angeles Riot Study: Riot Participation.* Los Angeles: Institute of Government and Public Affairs, University of California, 1967, pp. 20-21.

Seidenbaum, Art. *Confrontation on Campus: Student Challenge in California.* Los Angeles: Ward Ritchie Press, 1969.

Sharp, Gene. *Exploring Non-violent Alternatives.* Boston: Porter Sargent Publishers, 1970.

Shay, F. *Judge Lynch, His First Hundred Years.* New York: Ives Washburn, 1938.

Shellow, R. "Reinforcing Police Neutrality in Civil Rights Confrontations," *Journal of Applied Behavioral Science,* 1 (July-August-September, 1965), pp. 243-254.

Sherif, M. "A Study of Some Social Factors in Perception," *Archives of Psychology,* No. 187 (1935).

Sherif, M. and O. J. Harvey. "A Study in Ego Functioning: Elimination of Stable Anchorages in Individual and Group Situations," *Sociometry,* 15 (1952), pp. 272-305.

Shibutani, T. *The Circulation of Rumors as a Form of Collective Behavior.* Unpublished doctoral dissertation, University of Chicago, 1948.

_____. *Rumors in a Crisis Situation.* Unpublished Masters dissertation, University of Chicago, 1944.

Shils, Edward and Michael Young. ."The Meaning of the Coronation," *Sociological Review,* 1 (New Series, 1953), pp. 63-81.

Short, James R. and Marvin E. Wolfgang. *Collective Violence.* Chicago: Aldine-Atherton Press, Inc., 1972.

Silver, Alan. "The Demand for Order in Civil Society: A Review of Some Themes in the History of Urban Crime, Police and Riot," in *The Police: Six Sociological Essays,* David J. Bordua, ed. New York: John Wiley & Sons, 1967), pp. 12-13.

_____. "Official Interpretations of Racial Riots," *Urban Riots: Violence and Social Change, Proceedings of the Academy of Political Science,* 29:1 (July, 1968), pp. 146-158.

Simmel, George. "The Sociology of Sociability," *American Journal of Sociology,* (November, 1949), pp. 254-261.

Skolnick, Jerome. *Justice Without Trial.* New York: John Wiley, & Sons, Inc. (1966), pp. 96-111.

Smellie, K. "Riot," *Encyclopaedia of the Social Sciences,* 13, (New York: Macmillan 1935), pp. 386-388.

Smelser, N. J. *Theory of Collective Behavior.* New York: The Free Press, 1963.

Smith, Bruce L. R. "The Politics of Protest: How Effective is Violence?," in *Urban Riots: Violence and Social Change*, ed. Connery, R. H., Proceedings of the Academy of Political Science, Columbia University, 29:1 (Summer, 1968).

Smith, Dennis. *Report From Engine Company 82*. New York: Simon and Schuster, 1972.

Smith, G. H. "Beliefs in Statements Labeled Fact and Rumor," *Journal of Abnormal Social Psychology*, 42 (1947), pp. 80-90.

Smith, T. S. "Conventionalization and Control: An Examination of Adolescent Crowds," *American Journal of Sociology*, 74 (1968), pp. 174-183.

Smith, W. A. *Anglo-Colonial Society and the Mob, 1740-1775*. Unpublished Ph.D. dissertation, Claremont Graduate School, 1965.

Smyrl, Frank H. *Unionism, Abolitionism, and Vigilantism in Texas: 1856-1865*. Unpublished M.A. Thesis, University of Texas, 1961.

Snyder, David and Charles Tilly. "Hardship and Collective Violence in France 1830-1960," *American Sociological Review*, 37 (October, 1972), pp. 520-532.

Solnit, A. J. "Some Adaptive Functions of Aggressive Behavior" in *Psychoanalysis — A General Psychology*. New York: International Universities Press, Inc., 1966.

Somerville, H. M. "Some Cooperating Causes of Negro Lynching," *North American Review*, 177 (1903), pp. 506-512.

Sommer, Robert. *Personal Space: The Behavioral Basis of Design*. Englewood Cliffs, N.J.: Prentice-Hall, Inc., 1969).

Sonnichsen, C. L. *I'll Die Before I'll Run: The Story of the Great Feuds of Texas*. Revised Editions. New York: Devin-Adair, 1961.

_____. *Ten Texas Feuds*. Albuquerque, N. Mex.: University of New Mexico Press, 1957.

Sorel, Georges. *Reflection on Violence*. Hulme, T. E. and J. Roth, Translators. New York: Free Press, 1950.

Sorokin, Pitirim A. *Man and Society in Calamity*. New York: E. P. Dutton, & Co., Inc., 1942.

Speigel, John. "Social Psychological Impressions of a Riot," *Lemberg* Center for the Study of Violence, (1967).

Spilerman, Seymour. "The Cause of Racial Disturbances: Tests of an Explanation," *American Sociological Review*, 36 (June, 1971), pp. 427-442.

Stampp, K. M. *The Peculiar Institution: Slavery in the Ante-Bellum South*. New York: Alfred A. Knopf, 1956.

Stark, Margaret, et al. "Some Empirical Patterns in a Riot Process," *American Sociological Review*, 39 (December, 1974), pp. 865-876.

Stark, Rodney. *Police Riots*. Belmont, Calif.: Wadsworth Pub. Co., 1972.

Stinchcombe, A. L. "Institutions of Privacy in the Determination of Police Administrative Practices," *American Journal of Sociology*, 69:2 (September, 1962), pp. 150-161.

Stone, I. F. *The Killings at Kent State: How Murder Went Unpunished*. New York: Random House, Inc., 1971.

Strauss, Anselm. "Collective Behavior: Neglect and Need," *American Sociological Review*, 12 (June, 1947), pp. 352-354.

_____. "Research in Collective Behavior: Neglect and Need," *American Sociological Review*, 12 (1947), pp. 352-354.

Sudnow, David. "Temporal Parameters of Interpersonal Observation," *Studies in*

Social Interaction. New York: Free Press, 1972.

Swanson, Guy E. "Agitation in Face-to-face Contacts: A Study of the Personalities of Orators," *Public Opinion Quarterly,* 21 (1957), pp. 288-294.

_____. "A Preliminary Study of the Acting Crowd," *American Sociological Review,* 18 (1953), pp. 522-533.

_____. "Towards Corporate Action: A Reconstruction of Elementary Collective Process," *Human Nature and Collective Behavior.* Englewood Cliffs, N.J.: Prentice-Hall, Inc., 1970.

Swingle, Paule G. *Social Psychology in Natural Settings.* Chicago: Aldine Publishing Co., 1973.

Taylor, J. L. *Social Life and The Crowd.* Boston: Small, Maynard & Co., 1907.

Ten Houten, W. D. and C. D. Kaplan. *Science and Its Mirror Image.* New York: Harper and Row, 1973.

Thrasher, F. M. *The Gang.* Chicago: University of Chicago Press, Ltd., 1963.

Tiger, Lionel and Robin Fox. "The Zoological Perspective in Social Science," *Man,* 1:1 (March, 1966).

Toch, Hans. *the Social Psychology of Social Movements.* Indianapolis: The Bobbs-Merrill Co., Inc., 1965.

Torrence, E. Paul. "The Behavior of Small Groups Under the Stress Conditions of Survival," *American Sociological Review,* 19 (1954), pp. 751-755.

Trotter, W. *Instincts of the Herd in Peace and War: 1916-1919.* London: Oxford University Press, 1919.

Trotsky, Leon. *The Russian Revolution.* Garden City, N.Y.: Doubleday & Co., Inc., 1932.

Turner, R. H. "Collective Behavior," in *Handbook of Modern Sociology,* ed. Faris, R. E. (Chicago: Rand McNally, 1964).

_____. *Collective Behavior,* 2nd ed. Englewood Cliffs, N.J.: Prentice-Hall, 1972.

Turner, R. H. and L. M. Killian. *Collective Behavior.* Englewood Cliffs, N.J.: Prentice-Hall, Inc., 1957.

_____. "The Public Perception of Protest," *American Sociological Review,* 34 (December, 1968), pp. 815-831.

_____. "The Theme of Contemporary Social Movements," Presented at the annual meeting of the American Sociological Association, August, 1968.

Tuttle, W. M., Jr. *Race Riot, Chicago in the Red Summer of 1919.* New York: Atheneum, 1970.

United States Congress, House of Representatives, *Memphis Riots and Massacres,* Report No. 101, 39th Congress, 1st Session, Ordered Printed, July 25, 1866.

United States Riot Commission. *Report of the National Advisory Commission on Civil Disorders.* New York: Bantam Books, 1968.

United States War Department, War Plans Division. *Military Protection, United States Guards the Use of Organized Bodies in the Protection and Defense of Property During Riots, Strikes, and Civil Disturbances.* Washington, D.C.: Government Printing Office, 1919.

Vanderblue, H. B. "The Florida Land Boom," *Journal of Land and Public Utility Economics,* 3 (1927), pp. 113-131; 252-269.

van Gennep, Arnold. *The Rites of Passage.* Chicago: University of Chicago Press, 1972.

Vittachi, T. *Emergency '58: The Story of the Ceylon Race Riots.* London: Andre Deutsch, 1958.

Walsh, Richard. *Charleston's Sons of Liberty: A Study of the Artisans: 1763-1789.* Columbia, S.C.: University of South Carolina Press, 1959.

Wanderer, Jules J. "1967 Riots: A Test of the Congruity of Events," *Social Problems,* 16:2 (1968), pp. 193-198.

Weckler, J. E. and T. E. Hall. *The Police and Minority Groups.* Chicago: The International City Managers Association, 1944.

Weitz, Shirley, ed. *Non-Verbal Communication.* London-Toronto: Oxford University Press, 1974.

Weller, Jack M. "Current Sociological Approaches to Collective Behavior: Some Problems and Possible Solutions," Presented at annual meeting of American Sociological Association, Denver, Colorado, 1971.

Weller, Jack M. and E. L. Quarantelli. "Neglected Characteristics of Collective Behavior," *American Journal of Sociology,* 79:3 (1973), pp. 665-685.

Westley, William. *The Formation, Nature and Control of Crowds.* Canada: Defense Research Board, 1955.

White, Lynn, Jr. "The Spared Wolves," *Saturday Review,* 23 (Nov. 1954), pp. 32-33.

William, D. *John Frost: A Study in Chartism.* Cardiff, 1939.

———. *The Rebecca Riots: A Study in Agrarian Discontent.* Cardiff, 1953.

Wirth, L. "Ideological Aspects of Social Disorganization," *American Sociological Review,* 5 (1940), pp. 472-482.

Wolfenstein, Martha. *Disaster: A Psychological Essay.* Glencoe, Ill.: Free Press, 1957.

Wood, S. A. *Riot Control.* Harrisburg, Pa.: The Military Service Publishing Co., 1952.

Worsley, Peter. *The Trumpet Shall Sound.* New York: Schocken Books, 1968.

Wright, Charles R. *Mass Communication, A Sociological Perspective.* New York: Random House, 1959.

Wright, Sam. "Tactics, Strategies and the Anti-War Movement: A Consideration on the Success of Mass Demonstrations," Paper presented at the Pacific Sociological Meeting, June, 1971.

Yablonski, Lewis. "The Delinquent Gang as A Near-Group," *Social Problems,* 7 (Fall, 1959), pp. 108-117.

———. *The Violent Gang.* New York: Macmillan and Co., 1962.

Zaidi, S. M. "An Experimental Study of Distortion in Rumor," *Indian Journal of Social Work,* 19 (1958), pp. 211-215.

Zusne, Leonard. *Visual Perception of Form.* New York: Academic Press, 1970.

INDICES

AUTHOR INDEX

SUBJECT INDEX